EDWARDIAN POPULAR
MUSIC

EDWARDIAN
POPULAR
MUSIC

Ronald Pearsall

Rutherford · Madison · Teaneck
FAIRLEIGH DICKINSON UNIVERSITY PRESS

First American edition published 1975 by Associated University Presses, Inc.
   Cranbury, New Jersey 08512

Library of Congress Catalogue Card Number: 75-10734

ISBN 0-8386-1781-6
Printed in Great Britain

CONTENTS

LIST OF ILLUSTRATIONS

INTRODUCTION

THE EDWARDIAN AGE has been described as the flash epilogue to the Victorian, and it can be seen as a period of transition between the balmy 1890s and World War I. But certainly not in its popular music. There is something specific and special about Edwardian music, whether it is epitomised by *The Merry Widow* and other operettas or by Elgar.

Perhaps the most characteristic of Edwardian musical forms was the musical comedy, anticipated in 1892 with *In Town*, but which reached its full flowering in the decade and a half that preceded the war. Many of these musical comedies were self-consciously modern, using contemporary references and brand-names, though at the same time there was a plethora of escapist musicals using exotic locales. A common factor of the musical comedy was the minimal demand on an audience's intelligence. Here there was a sharp break with the Victorians: the Victorians were expected to make some effort, but the Edwardians were not. They belonged to a consumer society at its most self-indulgent.

We see this also in the music hall. The days of experimentation were gone. Audiences at variety theatres got what they wanted. Theatre management had found a formula and it took a lot to make them deviate from it. Often this was not due to lack of adventure on the part of management, but simply because production costs were staggeringly high. Audiences demanded favourite artistes doing their speciality pieces, and managers who were unwilling to pay the high salaries the stars demanded found that their patrons went elsewhere. In Glasgow, for example, Harry Lauder's salary was £1,000 a week—£10,000 in present-day money. Even minor artists in the provinces could command £200 a week not for any unique qualities but because the audiences had taken to them.

When a West End variety theatre paid out £2,000 a week in salaries, even when there were no big names, conservatism is understandable, and but for the absence of other entertainment media many unadventurous managements would have gone under. Although the Coliseum was renamed the Morgueseum by the cynical on account of its lack-lustre programmes, it kept going and still kept paying its shareholders fat dividends. If nothing better is offered, an entertainment-eager public will take what is going.

The Edwardian period saw the first flutterings of new forms of entertainment that were eventually to sink the music hall with all hands, the most significant of which was the cinema. The Bioscope and, later, the Kinematograph were acts on a music-hall bill, but few dreamed that they would soon start up on their own account. Not until the war period did the variety theatres suffer from the competition of the cinemas; but by 1917, 3½ million people were regular cinemagoers, *daily*.

That new, quaint and croaking instrument the gramophone did not harm the music hall or the musical comedy theatre. If anything, they complemented each other. The records made by a popular music-hall singer would be bought by an enthusiastic patron of, for example, George Robey or Albert Chevalier, and equally such records would send a buyer into the music hall to sample the comedian in the flesh.

In some areas of musical life, the advent of King Edward VII made little difference. Musical evenings were still a feature of middle-class life, and the question 'Have you brought your music?' was still answered in the affirmative. There were always sopranos and contraltos to sing 'Vilia' from *The Merry Widow* or baritones to tackle 'The Lost Chord'. Victorian ballads were as popular as ever, and there were hundreds of professional composers eager to keep up the supply. Amateur pianists were available in abundance, too, to rattle off their party pieces, though many were given a nasty jolt by the advent of the Pianola, the self-playing piano using perforated rolls. However, player-pianos, despite the enormous advertising stunts perpetrated on their behalf, never achieved the success that they had in the United States.

There was still a wide variety of outdoor music. The barrel-pianos were still a lively feature of the East End scene, hawkers and buskers continued to play every kind of instrument they could get their hands on from tuned bells to cornets, and the German bands paraded the streets, more musicianly than most but by no means more welcome. Municipal authorities offered an excellent range of open-air music in parks. The London County Council could draw on a pool of more than a hundred first-rate musicians, and over a year as many as ninety outside bands would be employed as well as these. Admirable concerts were provided by dozens of seaside councils.

The Edwardian age saw an upsurge in concert parties and the triumph of the pierrot, who replaced the nigger minstrel on promenades and piers. The prestige stores and hotels had their own string bands, and towards the end of the period the introduction of the tango brought in the 'thé dansant'. But although it seemed at the time that the tango was to revolutionise the dance-hall scene and afternoons at home, another import from the Americas was destined to have a far greater effect in the long run. Clues could be found at the beginning of the period—the production in 1903 of the all-negro opera *In Dahomey*, the appearance of a new dance, the cake-walk, and in 1909 the emergence of a popular walking-dance, the Boston. But these manifestations were nothing to the impact of ragtime. Musicians fumed over it, *Punch* made fun of it, and there were letters in *The Times* about it.

Ragtime was the most significant event in Edwardian popular music. Its perky syncopated rhythms and modern lyrics appealed strongly to the young, bored with the endless procession of musical comedies, contemptuous of the music hall and the popular ballad. Ragtime made almost every other form of popular music look old-fashioned, faded echoes of art music. This was not quite fair, for the Edwardian composers of popular music had a great gift for creating melody, but in 1913 the novel seemed more attractive than the merely pretty. The ragtime songs that created such a furore, such as 'Hitchy-koo', now seem as quaint as their sober contemporaries.

During the period there was a determined effort to re-establish 'genuine' popular music, and the Folk Song Society, established in 1898, did all it could to dethrone music-hall song and popular ballad (there was less animosity towards musical comedy, for many of the composer-members of the society wrote them). These efforts can be seen as part of a pattern to emancipate the common man from rubbish: the same thing was happening in literature, with cheap reprints of the classics by Collins and the Everyman Library and the subsidisation of the *Encyclopaedia Britannica* by the newspaper tycoons, while a number of popular weekly magazines such as *Pearson's*, *Cassell's* and *The Strand* tried to implant the idea of culture, making it gossipy and familiar. It was an attempt to realise the Victorian ideal that if the best were offered to the masses it would be accepted. This genuinely altruistic approach to help the socially underprivileged get a share of the treasures of the good life merits approval, but there was no question that in music it failed dismally. The poor did not want what their betters considered good for them, and there was so much money tied up in the entertainment industry that the folk-song revival ran into difficulties when it came to its propagation. Nevertheless, this revival did have an effect on music in education, and folk songs, spurious and genuine, were admitted to school curricula. Similarly, the revival of Tudor and Stuart instrumental music for the benefit of the masses was never really a viable proposition.

There were some musical activities that kept going against all the odds. Amateur choral societies continued to operate, though advances in public transport killed many suburban societies, and there was a good deal of resentment at grass-roots level of attempts made to refashion the old war-horses such as *The Messiah*. The introduction of new modernistic choral works into the programmes was also treated with suspicion, a suspicion shared by middlebrows when confronted with Stravinsky or Schoenberg, who made their debut before British audiences during the period.

The saga of the brass band movement continued. The south of England still resolutely refused to give it the attention that the north devoted to it. Cheap railway travel helped to foster the competitive spirit among brass-band and choral-society enthusiasts in the north of England, and but for the war such activities might well have spread over the entire country.

It is idle to speculate what would have happened had World War I not occurred, musically, socially, or politically. Nostalgia for the long golden summers of the Edwardians led to a spirited wartime revival of musical comedy with *Maid of the Mountains* and *Chu Chin Chow*, but ragtime merging into jazz, marched on, and semi-professional concert parties providing a social rather than a musical service were clearly here to stay and anticipated that post-war phenomenon, the Co-optimists. The music hall, reeling from the body-blow dealt by the cinema, managed to keep going, the shows loaded with patriotic fervour and laced with soldiers' tunes. A mediocre turn could guarantee vociferous applause by displaying the flags of the allied nations and a rendering of 'Tipperary'. Only when peace came did the impresarios of the music hall realise that things had changed drastically, and that the mixture as before was not good enough. Only when the cinema began to talk and sing did they think about putting up their shutters and making a profitable conversion to a talking picture house.

CHAPTER ONE

MUSICAL COMEDY

THE RECIPE FOR Edwardian musical comedy was: take £20,000,
add lavish decor, sumptuous costumes, a clutch of beautiful girls
and hummable tunes, and brew for 500 performances. The result
was a frothy meringue, sweet but unsubstantial.

Musical comedy came to England in 1892 with *In Town*, following the success of an American 'musical comedy drama' *My
Sweetheart* in 1884 and *Jack in the Box* (1887) by George R. Sims

*This array of street posters towards the end of the nineteenth century
clearly illustrates the way the musical stage was going, with* A Gaiety
Girl *demanding all the attention.*

Musical comedy was a logical extension of burlesque, and this scene from The Girl from Kays *would have many parallels in that once fashionable form.*

(author of 'Twas on the Bridge at Midnight') and Clement Scott, the drama critic.

Musical comedy was a logical extension of burlesque, a form of stage entertainment in which almost anything went, with the thinnest of holds on reality or the material that was being parodied. A leading exponent of burlesque was John Hollingshead, who described himself as 'a licensed dealer in legs, short skirts, French adaptations, Shakespeare, taste and the musical glasses'. The loose framework of burlesque made it possible to interpolate new material at any stage, and this characteristic was taken over by musical comedy.

There were two vital differences between the two genres. Musical comedy was self-consciously modern, dealing with up-to-date manners and mores, and it was presented in contemporary dress. Out were tights, spangles, and eccentric costumes. In were exotic dresses and exquisitely cut suits.

The principal figure behind musical comedy was George Edwardes. Edwardes had been earmarked for the army, but had failed his exams, had then done a stint in management in Leicester, and had caught the eye of D'Oyly Carte who made him acting manager of the Savoy in 1875. Gilbert and Sullivan comic opera ('burlesque in long clothes' said Hollingshead, manager of the Gaiety) gave Edwardes insight into what people liked, and after ten years at the Savoy, Edwardes took a half-share in the Gaiety.

The first show Hollingshead and Edwardes put on was *Little Jack Sheppard*, a burlesque with the celebrated Nellie Farren playing the female lead. Hollingshead left the Gaiety after the burlesque proved a roaring success, and Edwardes tried his hand at light opera. *Dorothy* did not do too well, though it did after it was sold to the Prince of Wales's Theatre for £1,000, and Edwardes went back to the tried and trusted burlesque.

The press had been quick to see that *In Town* was a token of the future. It was, declared the *Sunday Times*, 'a curious medley of song, dance, and nonsense, with occasional didactic glimmers, sentimental intrusions, and the very vaguest attempts at satirising the modern "masher" '. The music by Osmond Carr was 'tunefully sprightly'. To the *Sunday Sun* the new musical was the brightest, raciest, and spiciest musical entertainment in London, and the gossip writers in the theatrical and women's papers fell over themselves to describe the dresses. Other journalists saw *In Town* as a reflex of London life and doings, embodying the essence of the time, and saw reality in the cardboard caricatures pushed on to the stage simply because they were dressed in high fashion.

Management jumped on the bandwaggon. In 1893 the composer of the music of *In Town* wrote the music to *Morocco Bound*, presented at the Shaftesbury, which had real ducks in a pond and dialogue of the quality of:

'D'you like whiskey and sodah?'

'Yes.'

'Sodah I!'

Nevertheless, 295 performances were not to be sniffed at, and *A Gaiety Girl* (1894), replete with high life and actresses marrying into the aristocracy (reflecting reality—twenty-three Gaiety Girls did marry into the aristocracy), confirmed intuitions. The theatrical paper *The Era* considered *A Gaiety Girl* light, bright, and enjoyable, and the composer Sidney Jones found that he had acquired a massive reputation. *The Shop Girl*, almost belligerently modern in its use of brand-names—there were scenes set in Garrod's, 'the Royal Stores'—ran for 546 performances. The music was by Ivan Caryll and Lionel Monckton, who were to prove to be the stalwarts of Edwardian musical comedy.

The Shop Girl, *music by Caryll and Monckton, was resolutely modern in tone, and laid down a formula for success for the Edwardian to follow.*

But already there was a breakaway movement, and familiar locales 'embodying the essence of the time'—shops, London stores, Kensington garden parties, a stage within a stage—were ready to be discarded for the exotic. There were some who thought that the musical comedy of the *In Town* type was too lax and loose-limbed, that the paper-thin plots needed to be re-worked, and that W. S. Gilbert could show the writers of musical-comedy books a trick or two. The description 'a musical play' was first used for *The Geisha* (1896), which had a tighter plot revolving round the heroine who goes to Japan, puts on geisha costume and is put up for public auction, knocked down to a Japanese nobleman, but rescued in the nick of time by a British naval officer with the help of a real geisha. Comparisons with Gilbert and Sullivan's *The Mikado* were made: Owen Hall was no Gilbert, Sidney Jones was no Sullivan. But the patrons did not give it the thumbs down, and the oriental trappings were used for *San Toy*, with China as setting instead of Japan. Edwardes had also poked into ancient Rome for *A Greek Slave* with some success.

By the start of the Edwardian period it was clear that musical comedy, in all its forms, was due for a long run, and the latest venture into the east had turned up a winner—*A Chinese Honeymoon*, which had the longest run of a musical comedy to date at the Royal Strand Theatre under the auspices of Frank Curzon. It opened on 5 October 1901 and ran for 1,075 performances. It was not eclipsed until 1916 with *Chu Chin Chow*, the definitive descent into oriental spices. For those who feared that the Edwardian age would wreak havoc on the *status quo*, the immense success of *A Chinese Honeymoon* was very comforting, though there were some who found this success difficult to stomach, in particular George Edwardes, who felt that he had a proprietary right in musical comedy, and Sidney Jones, the composer of the music to the previous essays in oriental *kitsch*. The book of *A Chinese Honeymoon* was by George Dance, the music by Howard Talbot.

Sir George Dance—he received the knighthood when he gave £30,000 to save the Old Vic—was typical of a kind of man who flourished in music hall and the musical theatre. As a young man he had written 'His Lordship Winked at the Counsel' for G. H.

McDermott, and later 'Come Where the Booze Is Cheaper', a tune that was played by a Guards band one Sunday afternoon on the terrace at Windsor Castle and which attracted the attention of Queen Victoria. Lady Antrim was told to find out what the pretty air was, and the bandmaster had to think twice whether the queen should learn that she had been listening in ecstasy to a common music-hall song praising drink and that the words ran;

> Come where the booze is cheaper,
> Come where the pots hold more,
> Come where the boss is the deuce of a joss,
> Come to the pub next door.

Dance was also responsible for exploiting the talents of Little Tich in the show *Lord Tom Noddy*, but his fortune came not from writing music-hall ditties or musical-comedy librettos but from the bars of West End theatres, over which he held concessions. *A Chinese Honeymoon* brought Louie Freear to the notice of the

The plethora of musical comedies with oriental settings had an effect on dress and design, as can be seen in the art of Raphael Kirchner, better known for his postcard beauties. (Courtesy Victoria and Albert Museum)

Edwardian public, and gave Lily Elsie, later a cult figure when she played in *The Merry Widow*, her first taste of London success. The magnate behind *A Chinese Honeymoon*, Frank Curzon, was the son of a successful businessman in Chester who, having made his own fortune in tailoring, built the Piccadilly Hotel and restored the fortunes of the Strand (on the site where Strand tube station now stands). By 1903 Curzon controlled the following London theatres: Avenue, Camden, Coronet, Prince of Wales, Comedy, Criterion, Wyndham's, and the Strand. By himself, or in association with Edwardes, Curzon put on at the Prince of Wales's a large number of musicals including *Miss Hook of Holland*.

The composer of *A Chinese Honeymoon* was Howard Talbot (1865–1928), who had had a mixed career. Born in New York, Talbot set out to have a life in serious music, studying under one of the bastions of the English musical scene, Parry. *A Musical Chess Tournament* (1893) was dedicated to him. This piece, neither fish nor fowl, had six performances, three at Oxford and three at Kings Lynn. *Monte Cristo Junior* (1896) caused no commotion in theatrical circles, and *A Chinese Honeymoon*, the main song of which seems to have been 'Martha Spanks the Grand Pianner', was tried out in Hanley in 1899 before it made the West End two years later. There was no reason why it should have gone down so well, for it was certainly no better than a score of other musical comedies.

The implications were not lost on management. Quality did not necessarily mean success. The ingredients could be poured in with a reckless hand regardless of expense, and if the mood of the public was antipathetic nothing could save the show. It was soon found that certain theatres in precisely the same belt drew totally different audiences. Edwardes's two main theatres were Daly's and the Gaiety. A musical could flop at Daly's and be a roaring success at the Gaiety, and vice versa. With money as their god and no innermost doubts about quality, the Edwardian managers knew that they had to be ruthless. A musical with all the right things about it that was not going well had to be expunged from the register before it soaked up too much money.

The successful impresario had to be a gambler, sanguine when he had backed a loser, ready to cash in on by-products such as gramophone records and advertising revenue when a musical was raking in the money. George Edwardes was the most famous of these managers. He had a style of dress that marked him out from the crowd—a lounge suit with a top hat: he was as interested in horse-racing and the all-night card party as his theatres, and entertained largely at the Savoy and Romano's. He had no taste, and it was said by those who knew him, and not those starry-eyed embellishers of Edwardiana, that he had no inventiveness, no initiative, and no sparkle of personal wit. At rehearsals his high plaintive voice could be heard, 'No! No! I don't like that at all. Try something else.' But he rarely knew what he wanted as a substitute. That was the job of the tradesmen, the writer, the composer, the leading lady, the comic. Fortunately for Edwardes, he had a team who were thoroughly professional, who could make last-minute alterations to insert a topical subject, who could interpolate a comic song when the action was dragging, who could refurbish in minutes a sagging episode.

Sir Edward Moss.   Mr. George Edwardes.   Mr. Arthur Collins.   Mr. Charles Frohman.

"MANAGERS ARE CONSTANTLY DISCUSSING THE ADVANTAGE AND THE EXPENSE OF A NOVELTY."

Theatre managers constantly had to weigh up the advantages and expenses of a novelty. The running costs of a West End musical comedy were up to £2,500 per week. (Strand)

He was known affectionately as 'the Guv'nor', was recklessly extravagant with salaries and presents, but his contracts were like land-mines, deadly when not approached with caution. Everything was sacrificed for the main chance, and beneath the jollity and urbanity there lurked a calculating machine. One of his company told of an encounter between Edwardes and an old actor friend, meeting by chance in the Strand. 'Come along and see me one day,' invited Edwardes, 'I'd like to find something for you at the Gaiety!' 'But I've been there these three years!' pointed out the other.

There were two main sources of revenue following a successful London run—a provincial tour, and an American expedition. Throughout the period there was a considerable two-way traffic. Ever since *Belle of New York* had made a hit in London in 1898, creating a postcard celebrity in Edna May, entrepreneurs in America and Britain had realised the possibilities of two bites at the cherry. Even before, Edwardes had rushed off companies to Broadway for *A Gaiety Girl* and *The Geisha* in 1894 and 1897. Provincial tours were extremely profitable, and although even long-running shows could lose money in London these losses could be more than recouped by a company in the provinces. An impresario could have as many as sixteen touring companies on the road at any one time.

A key date in Edwardian musical comedy was 26 October 1903, when the new Gaiety was re-opened on the corner of Aldwych following the massive Strand redevelopment that swept away the slums around Drury Lane and was responsible for Kingsway. The occasion was patronised by King Edward VII and Queen Alexandra, and *The Orchid* brought a new face for idolisation, Gabrielle Ray.

The music of *The Orchid* was composed by Lionel Monckton and Ivan Caryll (1861–1921), real name Félix Tilkin, who had been responsible for the last show at the old Gaiety, *The Toreador*. Born in Liège, Caryll had studied music in Belgium before moving to London as an adaptor of French operetta. His own early work was not of much consequence, but in 1894 he met Edwardes who put him in charge of musical direction at the Gaiety. Caryll soon made his mark with *The Shop Girl* music, and readily assimi-

The Orchid *created a star in the previously unknown Gabrielle Ray. She became a 'postcard queen' overnight.*

lated the Edwardes philosophy and the importance of teamwork. His concept of the musical comedy was crisp and succinct—boy meets girl, sumptuous scenery and dresses, lively hummable tunes, no boring ensembles, two comedians, and a bevy of pretty ladies.

Having no regard for artistic integrity, Edwardes always stipulated in his contracts with his composers that additional musical material by whomever he pleased could be inserted into the text at any stage. Monckton and Caryll were professionally well equipped to deal with last-minute changes, and Monckton could be seen at the rehearsals sitting at a cottage piano off-stage waiting for his talents to be called upon. Instant musical composition is not a speciality of the present day. Lionel Monckton (1861–1924) had a much more distinctive style than Caryll and wrote a large number of memorable tunes for both musical comedy and operetta (though it is difficult to say where one ends and the other begins). He was largely responsible for *A Country Girl* (1902), though Paul Rubens interpolated the odd number, *The Cingalee* (1904), *The Quaker Girl* (1910) and *The Dancing Mistress* (1912). *Our Miss Gibbs* (1909) was shared with Caryll. Typical of the utterly charming tune that Monckton could produce was 'I'm Such a Silly When the Moon Comes Out' in *The Arcadians*, sung by Gertie Millar, a postcard queen *par excellence* and incidentally Monckton's wife (after his death, the Countess of Dudley).

Caryll had a longer list of credits, some of them good, some of them so-so, some of them abject failures—*Duchess of Dantzic* (1903), *The Girl From Kay's* (1903), another shop-floor musical trying to cash in on the success of its predecessor of the nineties, *The Cherry Girl* (1904), *The Little Cherub* (1906), and a couple of misses, *Chin-Chin* and *Nelly Neil*, both of 1907. America then took him, and this resulted in *The Satyr* (1910). The unenterprising titles give some idea of the stolid content, and extracts from the spoken business give some indication of the patchwork quality of the text. The following was reckoned by patrons of *The Orchid* as hilarious:

> Gertie Millar as low life heroine: I'm flaid.
> Fred Wright as Zaccary, low life hero: What art *flaid* about?
> Gertie Millar: I'm flaid you might kiss me!
> Fred Wright: How can I kiss thee wi' a can in other hand?
> Gertie Millar: I might 'old cans!

To typify the quality of the lyrics of the songs in *The Orchid* the following testifies:

> Liza Ann is a neat young lass
> And she's working up at Brigg's mill.
> Every morning at six o'clock,
> You can see her walking up the hill.
> There she goes with her turned-up nose
> And her dinner in a nice tin can,
> Oh, you'll all of you mad, when you see another lad,
> Is a-taking out Liza Ann!

Comparisons with the librettos and lyrics of W. S. Gilbert are superfluous, and one can gauge the humdrum and lack-lustre quality of such material by placing it against the costermonger songs of the music halls. Not that *The Orchid* was a particularly bad apple amongst a crate of good ones, though it merits especial attention as it was the show to open the new Gaiety with the king and queen in the audience.

One returns to the Monckton–Talbot *The Arcadians* for evidence that songs had not completely lost wit:

> See our dresses—every *one* done
> By the foremost firms in London,
> All their handwork is *un*done,
> Every shred!
> Swan from Edgar swims asunder,
> Stagg has got her mantle under,
> Pooles in puddles slip and blunder,
> Hope has fled.
>   (the 'Shower Chorus')

The Orchid ran for 559 performances (anything above 500 was very good indeed) and the aim of all management was to get as much mileage out of a show as possible. Edwardes had everything running for him at the Gaiety, a versatile, quick-witted comedian, George Grossmith, who could rattle the audiences as if they were rows of beads, a battalion of leading ladies each with a personal following, and the Gaiety Girls themselves, each one of whom could guarantee five or six regulars in the best seats. Edwardian beauty was there in abundance. It was of no importance that Gabrielle Ray could not act and her voice had a thin, piping quality. The appeal of the leading ladies and the girls was brought out by the elaborate dresses, hats, and coiffures. Cecil Beaton wrote that 'there was an intriguing perversity about such excess prettiness', and there was an element of the meat market in the stage productions of the Gaiety. The girls were there for the asking, though the price was usually high—marriage with an aristocrat. The Baroness Churston had been Denise Orme, née Jessie Smither, Countess Poulett had been Sylvia Storey, the Countess of Drogheda had been Olive May, née Meatyard.

The Orchid was succeeded by *The Spring Chicken*, adapted from the French by George Grossmith with music by Caryll and

Monckton, and there was a topical tie-up with the political *Entente Cordiale*:

> So come to France
> When you've a chance,
> You'll feel so gay when you are landing;
> Each girl you meet
> You'll find so sweet—
> There is a cordial understanding.

There was talk about a National Theatre, and that theme, too, was pumped into the text ('The day of the National Theatre/ Enthusiasts tell us is near'). *The Spring Chicken* enjoyed a back-

THE SUPPER.
Shall it be what she is accustomed to, or the best he can afford?

To be a musical comedy actress was to court a rich marriage. Each of the Gaiety Girls could guarantee half a dozen regulars in the best seats. A musical comedy star had access to Ascot, Goodwood, the best restaurants and the grandest houses in London. (London Magazine)

handed boost from an attack by the crusading journalist W. T. Stead on its alleged wickedness and indecency. Stead claimed that it glorified marital infidelity, but the attack served only as a plug for the show.

The Spring Chicken did well (401 performances), but Edwardes tried out a children's Christmas show which flopped, and the successor to *The Spring Chicken* flopped too, a return to old-fashioned burlesque with *The New Aladdin* and a principal boy in Lily Elsie. The music by Monckton and Caryll, with interpolated numbers by Frank E. Tours, did not save it, nor could they make its successor, *The Girls of Gottenberg*, into a major hit. Produced on 15 May 1907, it ran for 303 performances.

Monckton had also been busy doing the music for shows for Edwardes's other musical comedy theatre, Daly's. One of the few perspicacious critics, B. W. Findon of *Play Pictorial*, had realised that the best thing about *A Country Girl* (1902) was the music: 'The finest and most charming quality is its music, and particularly that of the first act, in which Mr Monckton has caught the real flavour of madrigal England.' There may be some doubt about this, but certainly Monckton's overture can still be heard now and then, and his consistently good music to the work has merited its occasional revival by amateur operatic societies.

Like his colleague Caryll, Monckton was no strumming hack. Educated at Charterhouse and Oxford, called to the Bar in 1885, music critic of the *Daily Telegraph*, he followed *A Country Girl* with *The Cingalee*, a farrago of nonsense set in Ceylon. It ran for 363 performances, a moderate success, but with the running expenses of Daly's being £2,500 a week anything marginal caused anxiety. For his next Daly's show, Edwardes went to France. Messager's *The Little Michus* has been described as a musical play or a comic opera, revolving round two girls who had got mixed up in a bath when a month old and whose identities, with the quaint logic of musical comedy, were therefore in doubt. Probably Edwardes thought he was venturing into high-class music, but *The Little Michus*, in the words of one of the songs, was, 'Only petticoats that rustle, rustle, with a frou, frou, frou, frou, frou'.

British management had had mixed fortunes with Andre Messager (1853–1929), though there was no question that he was

"LES MERVEILLEUSES" at Daly's Theatre

"La Merveilleuse"

SOME WALKING GENTLEMEN

MISS EVIE GREENE.

ST AMOUR (W H BERRY) AND THE POLICE AGENTS

PUZZLE: FIND Robert Evett !!

Mdlle Mariette Sully AND LOUIS BRADFIELD

Les Merveilleuses *was called by the cab-drivers 'The Marvellous 'Ouses',
and its English title,* The Lady Dandies, *did nothing to help. The
musical comedy formula could sometimes fail.* (The Bystander)

a talented composer. His ballet music often features in programmes of French music, though the average music-lover tends
to confuse him with Massenet. In 1894 Messager had written
Mirette for the Savoy, and this had been a failure. So was his
La Basoche, put on at the English Opera House to save it after
Sullivan's *Ivanhoe* had been given the thumbs down. But *Veronique*,
tried out by a French company at the Coronet Theatre, Notting
Hill Gate, had done well when transferred to the Apollo Theatre,
which was also under the control of George Edwardes. Though
no Daly block-buster like *A Country Girl* (729 performances),
The Geisha (760 performances), or *San Toy* (768 performances),
The Little Michus charted up 397 performances, and Edwardes
mined the same seam in *Les Merveilleuses*, called by the taxi-
drivers 'The Marvellous 'Ouses' and given the provisional and
unacceptable English title *The Lady Dandies*.

The disaster of its unpronounceable name and unexceptional
music by Hugo Felix (1872–1934), composer of *Madame Sherry*
(Berlin 1902, later London) and *Tantalizing Tommy* (1904) made
The Lady Dandies one of Edwardes's misjudgements. But
Edwardes could cope with mistakes. He had managed to forget
the fiasco of *The Duchess of Dantzic*, put on at the Lyric in 1903.
This had cost £15,000 before the curtain went up, and with a
chorus of sixty, an orchestra of forty, and music by Caryll, high
hopes had been entertained for it. It sank with all hands.

Edwardes, no matter how many fingers he had in the London
theatre pie, could not afford to let his competition wrest his
audiences from Daly's or the Gaiety. Rival impresarios were
only too eager to see 'The Guv'nor' biting off more than he
could chew, and the insouciant charm begin to fray at the edges.
It is interesting to examine what competition there was between
October 1902 and September 1903, just before the key date of
October 1903 when the new Gaiety was opened:

closing dates

Daly's: *Country Girl* (musical comedy)
         Tanner and Monckton   8 June 1902
Gaiety: *The Toreador* (musical comedy)
         Nicholls and Caryll   17 Jan 1901–4 July 1903

The Lyric Theatre never achieved the successes of Daly's or the Gaiety,
and Robin Hood was one of the shows that never quite made the grade.
(The Bystander)

closing dates

Strand: *A Chinese Honeymoon* (musical
              comedy) Dance and Talbot   5 Oct 1901
Apollo: *The Girl from Kay's* (musical
              comedy) Hall and Caryll   15 Nov 1902
Prince of
Wales: *Three Little Maids* (musical
              farce) Rubens   8 Sept 1902–25 Apr 1903
              The School Girl (musical farce)
              Hamilton and Stuart   9 May 1903
Savoy: *Naughty Nancy* (musical farce)
              Bath and Lyon   18 Sept–21 Nov 1902
              Merrie England (comic opera)
              Hood and German   24 Nov 1902–17 Jan 1903
              The Princess of Kensington (comic
              opera) Hood and German   22 Jan–16 May 1903
Lyric: *The Medal and the Maid* (musical
              comedy) Hall and Jones   30 Apr–18 July 1903
Shaftesbury: *In Dahomey* (negro opera)
              Spry and Cook   16 May 1903
Terry's: *My Lady Molly* (comic opera)
              Jessop and Jones   14 March 1903

Perhaps the most significant work, presenting ultimately a threat to the whole fabric of English musical comedy, was *In Dahomey*, with an all-negro cast and music and words by, reported *The Era*, members of 'the same interesting nationality'. This musical 'with its wonderful vitality, its quaint comedians, its catchy music, and its unique environment, should be one of the dramatic sensations of the London season'.

It is interesting to see Edward German's *Merrie England* having such a rough ride at the Savoy. Compared with the run-of-the-mill musical, *Merrie England* was reckoned to be intellectual entertainment. A hardy perennial for many an amateur operatic society, it had, and has, a number of merits, for Edward German (1862–1936) was a composer of talent, though, like Sullivan, he tried to straddle serious and light music. Although he did not write anything so ghastly as 'The Lost Chord', German (born

Edward German Jones) tried hard to catch the ear of the 'Lost Chord' public, perpetuate the work of Sullivan, and turn a pretty penny with *Merrie England*, *A Princess of Kensington*, and *Tom Jones* (1907).

German studied at the Royal Academy of Music, and became musical director of the Globe Theatre in 1888. His incidental music for *Richard the Third* in 1889 showed promise, and his *Henry the Eighth* music, composed for Henry Irving's revival of the Shakespeare play at the Lyceum, was considered outstanding. The familiar 'Three Dances' seemed to usher in a composer of importance, a master of pastiche, and in 1900 he was called upon to finish Sullivan's opera *The Emerald Isle* after several years of success as an accepted master of light music. Only two of Sullivan's numbers had been completed, though the melodies for fifteen more were in manuscript. It was admitted everywhere that a difficult task could not have been done better.

The plot of *Merrie England* concerned the love affairs of Sir Walter Raleigh, and Queen Elizabeth and the Earl of Essex were among the characters. On in November 1902, it was off less than two months later, despite the rollicking song 'The Yeomen of England' and 'The English Rose'. *A Princess of Kensington* incorporated 'Four Jolly Sailormen', but the plot was much too complex for an audience nurtured on unthinking mellifluity, and it did not do very well. Realising that in Edward German they did not have a natural successor to Sullivan, the Savoy management dropped him and German was obliged to go elsewhere to find a producer for *Tom Jones*.

However, German himself did not throw up the idea that he was another Sullivan, and in 1909 he collaborated with Sullivan's old associate on *Fallen Fairies* for the Savoy. This was based on a version of Gilbert's old play, *The Wicked World*, performed at the Haymarket thirty years before, and Gilbert had offered it to Sullivan, Elgar, Messager, Massenet, Liza Lehmann, and Alexander Mackenzie before German had been cornered. The fate of *Fallen Fairies* went to illustrate the fact that no matter how talented or illustrious the creators the public would give their work the thumbs down for reasons totally unconnected with quality.

At least German had not gone into the field of light opera/ operetta/musical comedy/musical farce/musical play with the notion that he was doing this mixed batch of genres a favour. He believed in what he was doing, and with a more sympathetic climate he would unquestionably have made more of an impact. Dismissed contemptuously as 'Olde-Englyshe-tea-shoppe', his music has at least had the dignity of numerous revivals, which is more than can be said of another 'classical' musician who went into the musical play field with the expectation of making a lot of money—Alexander Mackenzie.

Mackenzie (1847–1935) was one of a band of highly rated composers who were destined (it was believed) to bring a new glory to British music, part of the musical renaissance that included Stanford, Parry and Elgar. Among Mackenzie's works were an oratorio, several operas, a violin concerto and a piano concerto. Mackenzie believed that a formula could be found for the successful musical, and having done *His Majesty* for the Savoy, which failed, he set about writing one for the Edwardians. *Knights of the Road* (1905) made no impression at all; a musical comedy audience did not care whether a composer had a brace of operas, oratorios, and concertos to his credit. Perhaps it was typical of Mackenzie's detachment that when he heard a brass band playing a selection from his own *His Majesty* he turned to the composer Bantock and remarked 'You know, Sullivan has written some jolly good tunes.'

With this kind of attitude one does not regret Mackenzie's failure, though one can sympathise with Edward German. *Tom Jones*, with its charming 'Waltz Song', was a well-written, tuneful work, but any chances that it had were wrecked by the intrusion of the phenomenon that was to activate a complete rethinking of Edwardian musical comedy—*The Merry Widow*.

The Merry Widow was a social as well as a theatrical event. It was put on as a stop-gap by George Edwardes, pending the production of *The Dollar Princess*, and it had been performed at 450 European theatres before London was invited to see it. By 1907 it was clear that demand was exceeding supply. Edwardes had seen French light opera lose attention, and his band of faithful composers and librettists seemed to be losing their touch. The

The Merry Widow *was a social as well as a theatrical event. Put in as a stop-gap, it had been performed in 450 European theatres before London was invited to see it, and any actress who played the Widow had, as this illustration shows, the world at her feet.* Cassell's) Magazine)

public were jaded with the mixture as before, and it was not clear what they wanted: even musical expeditions to China had lost their lustre.

Die Lustige Witwe had been discovered by J. A. Malone in Vienna. Malone was Edwardes's manager and right-hand man, and had been searching the Continent for new ideas. *Die Lustige Witwe* was refurbished, the musical content was reduced and the comedy built up, and a new third act was put in. *The Merry Widow*, as presented at Daly's, was a triumph of fantasy over reality, the quintessence of the meringue, long-drawn-out sweetness with all the modernity of the first musical comedies, so admired by the theatre critics, forgotten.

Lily Elsie was cast as the heroine, and an American light comedian, Joe Coyne, was the hero. The composer was Franz Lehar, an ex-bandmaster in the Austrian army, and Viennese *kitsch* in a Paris setting made him a large sum of money—£60,000: the librettist earned £40,000. The formula had been found. *The Merry Widow* ran from 8 June 1907 until 31 July 1909 and was seen by 1,167,000 (almost as many as now watch a cultural programme on BBC 2). Edward VII saw it four times, and at one time it was being performed at over 400 theatres in Europe on the same evening. It was a European, not merely an English

West End panacea to all the ills and apprehensions of the age.

Before the run ended, 200,000 copies of the famous waltz were sold in Britain, Miss Elsie played the role more than 700 times, and the dance halls of England throbbed to the 'Merry Widow Lancers' and 'Merry Widow Quadrille'. There were other merry widows, anxious to sing 'Vilia', its runaway hit, but Lily Elsie enjoyed the lioness's share of the fame. There was a Merry Widow club in New York, there was a Merry Widow sauce, and the bells of the parish church of a little Dutch town were reset to play the Merry Widow waltz. The musical set a new fashion in hats, and created a craze for waltzes.

The last night was one of those theatrical occasions that nostalgia dotes on—all stalls sold for a guinea each and lovelorn gents offering thirty guineas for specific seats, queueing from 5.30 am, gallery queues full of quaint good humour standing nine deep and stretching 100 yards by kind permission of Edward Moss of the London Hippodrome, desirous of somehow getting into the act, and flowers everywhere.

There were some who looked askance at the undemanding entertainment epitomised by Lehar's masterwork. Osbert Sitwell as an Eton schoolboy saw it and later examined the phenomenon in relation to its time;

> It held a suitably designed mirror to the age, to the preference for restaurant to palace, for comfort to beauty, and to the idealization of Mammon. Mammon underlay the smudgy softness and superficial prettiness of the whole performance, as the skull supports the lineaments of even the youngest and freshest face.

The novelist Arnold Bennett felt that he *had* to see it 'in order to be *calé* [knowledgeable] on such things when it came to writing about London'.

> Same thing over again. Indeed I could notice no difference. Music even much less charming or superficially and temporarily attractive than I had expected. Troupe of about 40. Elaborate costumes, scenery, and appointments. Sylvia May,

Kate May, and the other principals, all chosen for their looks. Not one could avoid the most elementary false emphasis. Thus Sylvia May looking at a man asleep on a sofa, 'But *he* may wake up' (when there was no question of another man asleep) instead of 'He may wake *up*.' This sort of thing all the time. Also such things as recog*nize*. Three chief males much better. All about drinking, and whoring and money. All popular operetta airs. Simply nothing else in the play at all, save references to patriotism. Names of tarts on the lips of characters all the time. Dances lascivious, especially one. I couldn't stand more than 2 acts. Too appallingly bored.

It needed more than a dash of salutary cold water to calm down the public, and other Viennese works followed: Lehar's *The Count of Luxembourg* (1911), Oscar Straus's *The Waltz Dream* (1907) and *The Chocolate Soldier* (1908). But *The Count of Luxembourg* did not have the impact of *The Merry Widow*, nor did Lehar's subsequent concoction *Gipsy Love* (1912).

The adulation that *The Merry Widow* received conceals the fact that its London run was in no way extraordinary, even using Edwardian statistics. *The Arcadians* and *A Chinese Honeymoon* clocked up more performances: the run of *Chu Chin Chow* (1916) was three times as long. But the Lehar was a watershed. It was a relief to management that a new style had been found with a social cachet, that a public identified with. Moreover, *The Merry Widow* made few demands on anyone—except on the patience of killjoys like Arnold Bennett. There were no tricky bits in the music for suburban contraltos, rippling out 'Vilia', the most stumbling amateur pianist could get by with the waltz, and there was no intricate plot to puzzle the groundlings. Nor was there any history to dampen down enthusiasm.

Retrospection gets more acid as the years go by, and as those who fondly remember *The Merry Widow* get fewer it becomes easier to remember that the show did not dominate musical comedy until World War I. *The Dollar Princess* which followed it at Daly's was crammed with waltzes, but the setting of the third act—Freddy's Bungalow, California—was far removed from the Vienna–Paris hot-house. *Our Miss Gibbs*, music by Monckton and

The music from The Merry Widow *was widely played in drawing rooms and at musical evenings. 'Vilia' was a must for suburban contraltos and sopranos.* (The King)

Gertie Millar was the star of Our Miss Gibbs, *an Edwardian venture in topical realism.*

Caryll, brought back the contemporary scene with a mill girl (Gertie Millar, of course) serving in a West End store, the theft of the Ascot Gold Cup, and a set of the White City, the marvel of the Franco–British Exhibition, conjured up out of fibrous plaster. '*Enfin*', declared the editor of *Punch*, Owen Seaman, 'a very passable evening's distraction for those who are in the vein and a comfortable stall.' *The Sunshine Girl* (1912) brought in a thoroughly proletarian background, the thinly disguised Port Sunlight, and *The Girl on the Film*, though not a success, was unquestionably up-to-date, as was *The Girl in a Taxi*, which created a catchphrase —and this the *Widow* never did—'If you can't be good, be careful.'

The Arcadians (1909) was proof that there were other managements in musical comedy other than Edwardes. Robert

Courtneidge, who had backed German's *Tom Jones*, was apparently the only man who believed in it. It ran two and a half years in London, toured the provinces for another ten. The leading lady, Phyllis Dare, was paid only £45 a week; the girls in the chorus were on £2 a week. The jolly overture to *The Arcadians* is perhaps the best-known orchestral number from Edwardian musical comedy, beloved by light orchestras and military bands. 'I've gotter motter—Always Merry and Bright!' vied with the *Merry Widow* songs. Unfortunately Courtneidge followed *The Arcadians* with *The Mousme*, a Japanese piece with a sensational earthquake scene, and lost £20,000 on it, destroying his confidence in the musical theatre.

Nobody had the magic touch. One of the best of musical comedy composers, Leslie Stuart (1866–1928), never quite scored a hit, though his musicals, *The School Girl* (1903), *The Belle of Mayfair* (1906) with its show-stopping 'Decorate the Room with Roses Red', *Havana* (1908), and *Peggy* (1911) were as tuneful and intelligent as any. The managers, revered and lauded by dozens of forelock-touching devotees of Gaiety Girls, can be seen as

Phyllis Dare was the leading lady in The Arcadians, *a show that many believed would crumble but which turned out to be one of the best of them all.*

The caption of this cartoon reads 'Going to the Palace Theatre in 1910*'*
Motor cars, aeroplanes, and balloons were novelties that came and went'
but the musical comedy, was seemingly, for ever. (Strand)

men trying to find the magic ingredient, fumbling with stale
stereotypes, meandering through a continent's musical heritage
taking a bit here and a bit there, a touch of *chinoiserie* and a dash
of Strauss (not Richard, but Johann).

As Edward VII gave way to George V and the shadows of
world war loomed, as American dance rhythms made the four-
square and tripping six-eight tunes of traditional musical comedy
seem old-fashioned, there were more people to sneer and scorn.
Basil Hood, who had done the book for Edward German's
operettas and, ten years later, was treading the Viennese measure
trying to cash in on the success of *The Merry Widow* with the
faded *Gipsy Love* (1912), counter-attacked fiercely. 'We are told
by so-called artistic persons,' he declared, 'that musical comedy is
an abomination of which the theatre must cleanse itself. These
attacks are nearly always arrogant and frequently insolent, while
the ignorance of those who make them is amazing . . .'

In musical comedy the part was always greater than the whole. The passion for collaboration and the often undignified attempts of serious composers to break into the genre made it tempting for managers to deal out sections of a musical like a hand of whist to the eager, well aware that a runaway success could set them up for life. As *Punch* had it in a serial called 'The Evolution of a Musical Comedy':

> Straightway they come, responding to his call,
>   Racking their brains for notions up-to-date;
> Full of their past experience, and all
>   Anxious and willing to collaborate.
> For, in an entertainment of this kind,
>   'The more the merrier,' please bear in mind.
> If the dialogue's written by A,
>   The construction is managed by B;
>   Then the lyrics, no doubt,
>   Will be duly turned out
>   By the efforts of C, D, and E,
> For the music, melodious and gay,
>   That will linger in ev'ryone's head,
>   Some examples you try
>   Both of X and Y,
>   With additional numbers by Z.
> Oh, variety's certain to pay
> In the score of a musical play!

With everybody doing their own thing it is surprising that musical comedies were produced with a plot at all. Certainly a long-running show could change drastically. Messy bits that did not get audience response would be discarded in favour of new, perhaps more topical business. The dresses of *The Arcadians* were altered throughout its long run as certain modes such as the 'hobble skirt' went out of fashion or ceased to be worth commenting on by the comedian.

In many ways, Edwardian musical comedy had similarities with early Victorian opera. Musically, both were vehicles for popular songs:

Things with a tune that are easy to hum,
Persons superior call them 'tum-tum'.

Bishop's 'There's No Place Like Home' came from his opera *Clari: or the Maid of Milan*. Monckton's 'I'm Such a Silly When the Moon Comes Out' came from *Our Miss Gibbs*. Balfe's 'I Dreamt That I Dwelt in Marble Halls' came from *The Bohemian Girl*. 'Yip-i-addy-i-ay' was a last-minute comic interpolation into *Our Miss Gibbs*.

There continued to be resemblances to burlesque, with the story line discarded for an episode that owed its existence to the

The sensational Camille Clifford with her hour-glass figure became the rage of the West End in The Catch of the Season *and* The Belle of Mayfair. (The Bystander)

passing whim of the producer or comedian, and did not have to
be clever or apposite:

What use in writing subtle epigram?
The line that gets most laughter is a 'Damn!'

The managers would have considered it unfair for a later
generation to look at a musical without taking notice of the decor,
the costumes, and, of course, the handsome men and pretty
women. When the action dragged and the music was going on
that bit too long there were always the girls to ogle. But we cannot
be turned on by a mere recital of women's names, as the 1920s,
1930s, 1940s and even the 1950s, were. Marie Studholme, Ada
Reeve, Ellaline Terriss, even the sensational Camille Clifford who
caused a furore with her hour-glass figure and, as the 'Gibson
Girl' in *The Catch of the Season* (1904), became the rage of London,
all these, with seemingly interchangeable faces, seem insipid compared with the lively ladies of the music-hall stage. The men,
with sleek hair, expressionless faces, and a range of puppet-like
gestures, dressed in immaculate evening dress, superbly cut
lounge suits, or form-flattering uniforms, have slipped even
more out of sight, and only the comedians, such as the long-
serving George Grossmith, emerge from history with any kind
of life.

Only the tunes have saved Edwardian musical comedy from
utter oblivion. But the tunes have been endowed with extra
vitality by their nostalgia content, by their wide dissemination by
gramophone, pier and Palm Court orchestra, and by radio. When
radio came in, in the 1920s, the musical comedies had been produced the day before yesterday, and because yesterday had been
the period of the great war, *The Merry Widow* and its contemporaries were tokens of a lost age, a glamorous age full of love and
laughter gone for ever.

CHAPTER TWO

MUSIC HALL

MANY OF THE features of Edwardian music hall could have been anticipated by the Victorians. In 1878 a law was passed demanding a certificate of suitability for music halls and variety theatres. This meant a proscenium wall dividing the stage from the auditorium, the installation of a safety curtain, and the sale of liquor abolished in the body of the hall. The smaller theatres could not afford to pay for the alterations, and closed: these included many of the pioneer music halls, and over the country 200 variety theatres and music halls were forced to put up their shutters, often remaining derelict until taken over as warehouses or mission halls. A few of the provincial halls staggered on, accommodating themselves to the situation as best they could, eventually to fall to the cinema boom, which gave suburban and provincial theatres a new lease of life.

With the act of suitability, a rationalisation of the whole music-hall industry began, and syndicates were formed. Chains of Hippodromes and Empires were built, larger and more comfortable than their predecessors, but demanding more of the performers. Even a third-rate artist could play upon an intimate audience in a small hall, but the atmosphere was lost when he was faced with an audience of thousands instead of hundreds, and there was no chairman to act as a link-man between stage and auditorium. A capable chairman was able to save a music-hall turn by acting as a straight man or feed to a suffering

The Royal Theatre of Varieties in High Holborn was typical of the large music hall that ousted the smaller intimate halls, although, unlike the Hippodrome or the Coliseum, the programmes of 1901 were very much the mixture as before. (Courtesy Victoria and Albert Museum)

The Empire, Bristol, was a characteristic product of the syndicates, a music hall using star performers operating on a circuit.

comedian, or interpolating his own contribution when a sequence was going badly.

In the changed conditions, a music-hall performer had to be good to survive, but the really first-rate artists found themselves in a position that the performers of the mid-Victorian period would have envied. They were so much in demand that they could ask almost any fee. Music-hall magnates, desperate to keep their audiences, entered into reckless competition with others of their kind, and committed themselves to immense outlay. Frequently they misjudged the quality of a performer, and there were mediocre artists drawing large salaries and contracted to do so for many years to come. With the wealth to be made from the new huge music halls, many of the old school went on longer than they should have done, and, aged and toothless, they mouthed their speciality songs to a bewildered audience which expected something rather better.

Popular music-hall turns knew their value, as the actor William Farren had done when the manager Alfred Bunn (1796–1860) had been reluctant to fall in with his wage demands. 'When there is only one cock salmon in the market you must pay the price,' said Farren. 'I am the cock salmon.' Wearily, Bunn paid up. Public demand was all.

In the early days of the music hall there was uncertainty about what the public wanted, whether it should have what it wanted or what the manager wanted, and what a viable wage for a music-hall performer should be. The performers managed their own affairs, and realised their value only when they went on tour or were approached by rival theatres. A comedian or singer could carry on for years at £5 a week, little knowing that his market value was perhaps £40 a week.

By the time Edward VII arrived on the throne, all this was ancient history. The managers knew what they wanted, the public knew what it wanted, and the performers used agents to get them the best deals. The public wanted big names singing the songs that made them famous or doing their speciality acts: they did not want to be improved, and preferred the tried-out favourites to newcomers. An artiste not even of the first rank, such as R. G. Knowles, could sing the same song for three months at a stretch, knowing that each time the hall would be crowded just to hear him sing it.

Unquestionably music hall had passed its peak. All forms of entertainment must suffer when money becomes the sole criterion, and the drive and the verve that characterised the best of Victorian music hall were mostly lost in the quest for universal appeal. The emphasis on family entertainment and the rapid decline of comic material in bad taste led to vapidity, and although certain talented performers transcended their material, in far too many of the music halls it was very much the mixture as before, and playing safe. The songs that had won their way into the public's heart were endlessly plugged, the sheet-music publishers, the impresarios, and the performers were all well recompensed; less often were the lyric and song writers. The songs were also played by the purveyors of mechanical music; during the Edwardian period these included the newly fledged gramophone, the disc musical box, the Pianola, and the barrel-piano.

At the start of Edward's reign, the following music halls were in operation in London: the Alhambra in Leicester Square, the Cambridge in Commercial Street, the Canterbury in Westminster Bridge Road, Collins's in Islington (the last to close), the Empire Leicester Square, the Hippodrome in Cranbourne Street, the

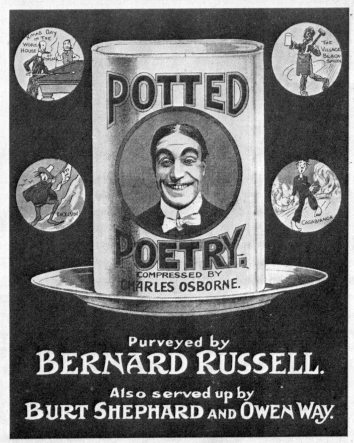

*The Edwardian music halls absorbed a vast mass of material, and
'Potted Poetry' of 1907 was one of the songs that fell by the wayside,
soon forgotten in favour of something more topical.*

The Alhambra *in Leicester Square retained its popularity, the management shifting its programmes about to cater for fads and fashions. At the time this photograph was taken wrestling was in vogue.* (Around London)

Metropolitan in Edgware Road, the Middlesex in Drury Lane, the Oxford in Oxford Street, the Palace in Cambridge Circus, the Paragon in Mile End Road, the London Pavilion in Piccadilly Circus, the Royal in High Holborn, the South London in London Road, and the Tivoli in the Strand. These were joined in 1904 by the dream music hall, the Coliseum, the brain-child of Oswald Stoll, which cost £80,000 more to build than had been predicted, and had a triple revolving stage that could be rotated at 20 mph and 10,000 square feet of stage.

The Coliseum contained an information bureau, a telephone kiosk, and a letter box. Also a glass tram running on lines directly to the Royal Box, a device that was not entirely successful. The Coliseum opened with two distinct programmes each day, programme one 12–2 and 6–8, programme two 3–5 and 9–11. Stoll was taken to task on the spelling of Coliseum—'I see you have knocked the "O.S." out of "Collosseum" ' to which the manager riposted, 'I've knocked the "O.S." out and put "I" in!', repartee about on the level of his comedians' patter, for the Coliseum was soon known as the Morgueseum. The programme motto 'Pro Bono Publico' did not impress the paying customers.

Although the Coliseum did not get off to the anticipated start,

The Palace Theatre in Cambridge Circus had been built as an opera house for the production of English opera, but it was as a variety theatre that it succeeded. (Around London)

Stoll had other theatres throughout London and the United Kingdom. The circuit system of sending stars from hall to hall meant that certain performers could earn immense salaries, though it also meant that comedians who cracked a blue joke at a far-off hall could be penalised by being blacked by the circuit. Another important impresario was Edward Moss, whose major property was the London Hippodrome, opened in 1900, and which could double as a water tank for aquatic entertainment or as an arena for spectaculars of the kind later a speciality of the Coliseum. To counter the effect and the buying potential of the Moss and Stoll chains, previously independent music halls formed a syndicate. The remaining halls, such as the Britannia in Hoxton or the Metropole, Camberwell Green, were at a disadvantage, not having the capacity to employ those artists that the public so wanted to see.

There were many who wondered how music halls could make

a profit considering the high cost of running them. That they did
is evident from the dividends paid to shareholders. In 1901 Moss
paid 12½ per cent, the Pavilion 9 per cent, and the Oxford 12
per cent. The salary list of the Hippodrome was reckoned at up
to £3,000 a week. Moss himself was asked how the Hippodrome
could make a profit:

> In connection with the London Hippodrome it has not been
> our plan to stint expenses in any way where we have had an
> opportunity to produce a spectacle which should warrant
> an elaborate *mise en scène*. Things are different now [1911] to
> what they were half a century ago. Music-halls are now not
> looked at askance as they were. The class of entertainment
> submitted to the public is higher than it has hitherto been,

AN "EMPIRE" BALLET.

*Expensive productions were required by a public 'which had been educated
up to a higher standard', and ballet played a considerable part in music-hall
programmes.* (Ludgate)

Managing Director · · Mr. ALFRED BUTT

2/5/1910

Programme - - 6d.

The Management politely request that where necessary Ladies will remove their hats in order not to obstruct the view of those sitting behind.

1.	Marche Russe	*Ganne*	8.0
2.	**MISS LILY HAYES** Comedienne		8.5
3.	**VICKEY DELMAR** Novelty Dancer		8.15
4.	**CHRISTIE DUO** Eccentrics		8.25
5.	**SELBO** Club Juggler		8.35
6.	**THE PALACE GIRLS**		8.50
7.	**LA CONTADINA** Italian Violinist		9.0
8.	**ALBERT WHELAN** The Australian Entertainer		9.10
9.	**THE GREAT GOLDIN** With a Series of New Illusions Assisted by Mdlle. JEANNE FRANSIOLI and Company		9.30
10	Orchestral Selection— "The Jumble Sale" ... *Arranged by Herman Finck*		9.50

MATINEE OF THE FULL EVENING PROGRAMME SATURDAY NEXT AT 2.
BOX OFFICE open from 10 a.m. to 11 p.m. TELEPHONE No. 6834 GERRARD (2 lines)

11.	**MISS MARGARET COOPER** and her Piano The Pianoforte by CHAPPELL.	10.5
12	**SAISON RUSSE**	10.25

Of Artistes from the Imperial Russian Ballet of St. Petersburg and Moscow
Special Engagement and First Appearance in England of

ANNA PAVLOVA and MICHAEL MORDKIN

Russia's acknowledged greatest Dancers and the famous Leaders of the
Imperial Russian Ballet
Supported by a specially selected Company of Premières Danseuses
For Programme of Dances see Special Slip

13.	**"KINEMACOLOR"**	11.0

The Natural Color Kinematograph Co., Ltd.—Urban-Smith Patents.

Paris, the Gay City | Choosing the Wallpaper

"URBANORA" BIOSCOPE.

Arrival of Lord Kitchener at Southampton | Mr. Grahame White's Great Aeroplane Flight Punchestown Races

Incidental Music by HERMAN FINCK.

MONDAY NEXT, MAY 9th
MISS CLARICE VANCE
In Renditions of Southern Coon Songs

Owing to the enormous demand for Seats a
SECOND SPECIAL MATINEE
Will be given WEDNESDAY NEXT, MAY 4th, at 3 o'clock
ANNA PAVLOVA and MICHAEL MORDKIN
Supported by a specially selected Company of Premières Danseuses
On this occasion several additional Dances not possible in the Evening Programme will be presented
GWILYM WIGLEY, the Celebrated Welsh Tenor, and ALBERT WHELAN,
The Australian Entertainer, will appear at this Matinee.
Seats can now be Booked   Doors open at 2.30   No Smoking Allowed

Musical Director—Mr. HERMAN FINCK   Stage Manager—Mr. FRANK DAMER
Acting Manager—Mr. E. A. PICKERING   Treasurer—Mr. M. E. BENJAMIN

NOTICE.—The Public can leave the Theatre at the end of the performances by all exit and entrance doors which open outwards. All gangways, passages and staircases must be kept free from chairs or any other obstructions. Persons must not be permitted to stand or sit in any of the intersecting gangways, and if standing be permitted in the gangways at the sides and rear of the seating, sufficient space must be left for persons to pass easily to and fro. The safety curtain must be lowered about the middle of the performance so as to ensure its being in proper working order.
The order and composition of this Programme may be varied as circumstances require.

During the Overture a Series of Pictures are shown by the World's Advertising Co., Ltd., of 248, High Holborn, W.C.

The Palace Theatre brought Pavlova to the notice of the British public. It is ironical that she is flanked on the programme by the device that killed the music hall—the kinematograph. (Courtesy Victoria and Albert Museum)

and more people are going in for this class of amusement
than at any time before.

The manager of the Coliseum in 1911, Dundas Slater, was of
much the same opinion. He considered that expensive productions were required by the public, 'which has been educated up
to a higher standard', and were better for all concerned. Certainly
lavish productions could command higher admission prices,
though the attempt by Stoll to give the music hall a new image
by making all seats at the Coliseum bookable backfired. The sixpenny public was not used to the innovation, and the booking
office could not cope with the flood of anonymous postal orders.
A chartered accountant was brought in to sort out the mess,
which he did by giving a ticket to anyone who said that he or
she had sent a postal order in. A subtle indication of Stoll's desire
to make the music hall respectable was his renaming of the
gallery—'balcony' had a much loftier ring.

An Empire production of a ballet *Round the World* was costed
by a journalist Jerrard Grant Allen. After the initial setting up
(at least £5,000) he estimated the weekly expenses as follows:

	£
Ballet, chorus, etc	360
Salaries in front of house	246
Wages, gas and electricity men	54
Wages, stage hands	310
Salaries, variety artistes	925
Orchestra	163
Wages, programme and cloak-room attendants	19
General incidentals	30

The West End music halls and variety theatres would try anything if it made money, and it is significant that managers who
came into the theatre from business were often more successful
than those bred in the theatre. Typical of the outsiders was
Alfred Butt, manager of the Palace from 1904, who began as an
accountant at Harrod's. Like the Alhambra, the Palace did not

start life as a music hall, but as the first home of English opera,
foundering on Sullivan's *Ivanhoe* in 1891. The Palace not only
brought Pavlova on to the English stage, but also La Polaire,
billed as the ugliest woman in the world who did an Apache
dance to the *Merry Widow* waltz: not only Maud Allan whose
semi-nude artistic dancing caused a furore, but also the 'classic'
dancing of Lady Constance Stewart-Richardson. Straight actors
such as George Alexander and Beerbohm Tree made their
appearance on the variety stage, tantalised by Butt's offer of
£750 a week.

The water-tank incorporated in the decor of the Hippodrome
was capitalised on by the management, and Annette Kellerman,
an Australian swimmer, created a revolution in women's swim-
wear. Clad in a blue jersey, knickers, stockings, and scarlet cap,
she rendered the knee-length costume obsolete overnight. To
make use of the vast stage, a massive tableau was created depict-
ing a Hyde Park scene, and using 12 horses and their riders, 4
motor-cars, 2 broughams, and 150 actors and actresses.

It might well be asked who would want to see such a charade
on a music-hall stage when a short omnibus ride would take
them to the actual site. Or why should a girl in a swimming
costume attract paying customers (even though Miss Kellerman
was attested to have the perfect figure). Or why a simulated
Derby at the Coliseum should be worth crossing London to see.
In an age which was acknowledged to be immoral but never
indecent, it is easy enough to see why scantily-dressed women
drew an audience, but for the rest of the spectaculars the only
answer can be the lack of any opposition, and the special position
the music hall enjoyed as a provider of entertainment to the mass
audience. It did not have this exclusiveness for long, and the
music hall and variety theatre managers, spending thousands of
pounds for vulgar and meretricious effects, had a rude awakening
from their complacency when the cinema ceased to be an amusing
titbit on one of the bills and came of age. As we have seen, by
1917 3½ million people were regular cinemagoers, daily.

Many of the music-hall impresarios had forgotten that what
they managed were not conglomerations of devices to dazzle a
goggling audience but halls for music. But the public had not

Scantily dressed women always drew an audience, and the Australian swimmer Annette Kellerman in her close-fitting costume was the logical successor to this can-can dancer of the 1890*s.*

forgotten. Those who went to see miracles of stagecraft and ingenuity were few compared to those who worshipped a select number of stars and their specialities.

By the twentieth century, many of the legendary figures of Victorian music hall had died or had left the halls. Jolly John Nash (1830–1901) had been known for his 'Sister Mary Walked Like That'; Arthur Lloyd, one of the Lions Comiques, had made his London debut in 1862 but his big song 'Not for Joseph' was still sung by others (Lloyd died in 1904); Jenny Hill and Nelly Power had started as child singers in the 1860s, and shared the kudos of one of the best of all music-hall songs, 'The Boy I Love Is Up in the Gallery'. Nelly Power was one of the first of the male impersonators, anticipating Vesta Tilley and Ella Shields. Jenny Hill died in 1896, Nelly Power in 1887. Bessy Bellwood was one of the first lady singers of Cockney songs, renowned for her 'What Cheer 'Ria' of 1887. She died in 1896 before she was forty. Although he lived to 1923, James Fawn, of 'If You Want to Know the Time, Ask a P'liceman' fame, was in his fifties when the new century broke.

The songs lived on after their creators and exploiters were dead. The songs somehow embodied the sentiments and feelings of the submerged classes, and the idea that music-hall song was the only true urban folk art gained credence throughout the Edwardian period. The ephemeral and the phoney—the songs tagged to a contemporary event or the uplift songs so beloved of members of the old school such as Harry Clifton—were forgotten, and those that illuminated or truly reflected some aspect of working-class life were kept afloat by battalions of diligent troupers.

The sentiment and simple feeling of 'The Boy I Love Is Up in the Gallery' was perpetuated by other performers after the Misses Hill and Power had died. It was one of the many songs of Marie Lloyd, whose first big hit came with 'Oh, Mr. Porter'. Born in 1870 in Peerless Street, Hoxton, Marie Lloyd also immortalised 'Then You Wink the Other Eye', 'Twiggy-voo' (giving a catchphrase to a nation), 'A Little of What You Fancy Does You Good', and 'One of the Ruins That Cromwell Knocked about a Bit'. T. S. Eliot described her as 'the most perfect, in her own style, of British actresses'. Other music-hall stars of the period he categorised as 'grotesques', one of whom was Nellie Wallace (1870–1948), a character rather than a singer, and whose songs are mostly forgotten.

If an audience accepted an artist they would stomach puerile rubbish. There were no guide-lines that a performer could follow to guarantee such acceptance, though a gimmick was a help. G. H. Chirgwin's was his cognomen, the 'White-eyed Kaffir'. An exile from the world of nigger minstrelsy, Chirgwin happened to rub his eye one day before going on stage and appeared before his public with a white patch in his black make-up. In subsequent performances he made this amorphous patch into a neat lozenge. Chirgwin used what became a Chaplin trick of diving between pathos and humour, but it was never pathos with an undercurrent of cynicism, but undiluted saccharine. 'The Blind Boy'

Many Victorian per-formers found it difficult to make the transition into the twentieth century, though Marie Lloyd was more fortunate than most. (Ludgate)

MISS MARIE LLOYD.

and 'My Fiddle Is My Sweetheart' were his two standbys, and mercifully these have not been resurrected by music-hall revivalists.

Many of the music-hall stars had done their apprenticeship in the small, cosy Victorian halls and had made the transition to the mammoth Edwardian variety theatres through professionalism and guts. Charles Coborn was one of these, starting his music-hall career at the Alhambra—not the Alhambra, Leicester Square, but the Alhambra, Isle of Dogs—doing two nights a week for half a crown. Born McCallum, Coborn took the pseudonym when standing on the corner of Coborn Road, Bow. From the Alhambra he moved to the Sugar Loaf Tavern in Whitechapel and other East End dates, the provinces, then to the celebrated Middlesex Music Hall (the Mogul, or the Old Mo) in 1879. Renowned for 'Two Lovely Black Eyes' (1886) and 'The Man

Who Broke the Bank at Monte Carlo' (1891), Coborn was a shrewd businessman, buying the rights of the latter song from the songwriter Fred Gilbert for £10, asking Francis, Day & Hunter £30, and agreeing on £5 down and a royalty—which netted him £600. In 1907 he was one of the leading figures in the strike of music-hall artistes for better pay.

Harry Randall (1860–1932) was not able to move with the times, and his songs, such as 'It Ain't All Lavender' and 'Oh, What a Night It Must Have Been', did not have the lasting power to be passed on to a new generation. Dan Leno died young, just squeezing into the Edwardian period. Starting life as a clog-dancer, and proclaimed after a six-day contest as 'Champion Clog-dancer of the World', Leno appeared at the Middlesex in 1885 as an Irish comic vocalist and clog-dancer. One of T. S. Eliot's grotesques, Leno was as much an impersonator as a singer, and the titles of his songs reflect this. He performed before the Prince of Wales, and this went to his head; expecting to be at least ennobled, he died deranged in 1904, not realising that Edward's patronage was not important. Jolly Jack Nash could equally have expected some kind of honour, for he performed before the newly crowned king, who joined in the chorus:

Hey, hi. Stop, waiter! Waiter! Fizz! Pop!
I'm Racketty Jack, no money I lack,
And I'm the boy for a spree!

Not inapposite words for his majesty to sing.

Like Chirgwin, Eugene Stratton (1861–1918) was a black-faced singer, finding that they still had novelty appeal to a pre-Black-and-White-Minstrel age. Considerably more talented than Chirgwin, Stratton, 'the Whistling Coon', was associated with the old Oxford, Tottenham Court Road. An expert song-and-dance man, Stratton was fortunate enough to become friendly with Leslie Stuart who was predominantly a musical-comedy writer, and it was for Stratton that Stuart composed two of the best-known music-hall songs, 'Little Dolly Daydream' and 'The Lily of Laguna'. As a writer, Stuart had a vein of musical adven-

Music-hall songs and ballads could be ludicrous out of their setting. (Cassell's Magazine)

Street Hawker (*crying his songs*):
" ' 'OW'D YER LIKE TO SPOON WID ME?'
' IN THE SHADE O' THE OLE APPLE TREE.' "

ture rare in the genre, and his song rhythms have a rakish agility and a quirkishness that one does not come across until the post-war days of Gershwin and Cole Porter. Perhaps Stuart's most characteristic song comes not from the music-hall repertoire but from musical comedy—'Tell Me, Pretty Maiden' from *Florodora*. Many a dance-hall busker has come to grief on this delightfully treacherous tune (perhaps the best of its kind ever written).

If there was one category of song that the music-hall audience adored it was pseudo-Cockney. The Lions Comique of the 1860s had made something of a speciality of topographical songs dealing with London, but these were brisk and sardonic and the locations were incidental. The late Victorian and Edwardian Cockney songs were different altogether, successfully marrying humour and pathos and dealing with real situations that the lower and lower-middle classes could identify with. The 'Laureate of Costerdom' was reckoned to be Albert Chevalier. Chevalier was certainly no East End barrow-boy who had happened to leave his pitch outside a Whitechapel penny gaff, but a fully-fledged actor. Under the name of Knight he appeared in a production by the Bancroft husband-and-wife team in 1877 of *An Unequal Match*, and later played in Pinero farces at the Court (later the Royal Court) Theatre. He was thirty when he adopted his costermonger *persona*, and although anyone who had worked under the aegis of the Bancrofts could hardly avoid hamming it up at times, the personification was well-nigh perfect. The world is unquestionably richer through 'Knocked 'Em in the Old Kent Road' and 'My Old Dutch'. A verse from a less well-known song, the 'Coster's Serenade', gives some idea of the vein of material Chevalier worked:

> You ain't forgotten yet that night in May,
> Dahn at the Welsh 'Arp, which is 'Endon way.
> You fancied winkles and a pot of tea.
> 'Four ale', I murmured, ' 's good enough for me.
> Give me a word of 'ope that I may win'—
> You prods me gently with the winkle pin;
> We was 'as appy as could be that day,
> Dahn at the Welsh 'Arp, which is 'Endon way.

A contemporary of Chevalier and a fellow miner in the same rich seam of humour and Cockney romance was Gus Elen (1863–1940), famous for 'It's a Great Big Shame' and 'If It Wasn't for the 'Ouses in Between'. Elen played it cool and did not milk the audience for laughs: despite his merits he is inclined to be overshadowed by Chevalier and Harry Champion who, although only three years younger than Elen, seems to belong to a later generation, probably because of the records he made between the wars. Harry Champion, more than anyone, was a link between the quickfire patter comedians of the high Victorian era and those of today.

Scorned by purists, Harry Champion illustrates all that was best about Edwardian song and singers. He made his debut as Will Conway, a black-faced comic, in 1888, and, unlike Dan Leno, for example, who had aspirations above his station and lived a genteel life, Champion was all of a piece. His stage *persona* reflected his real self—beery, red-nosed, and loud. When so many

The London music-hall audience appreciated local references. 'Dahn at the Welsh 'Arp which is 'Endon way' was an Albert Chevalier speciality.
(Around London)

of the Edwardian Cockney singers had soft centres, the hard nut that was Harry Champion comes as a refreshing relief. As with George Leybourne, the 'Great' Vance, and G. H. McDermott, the Lions Comique of the previous generation, Champion was a true professional with unequalled command of the high-speed song, the words of which were ironical and crusty. He was the man who could sing six songs in two minutes and get paid for it.

His song 'Any Old Iron' is perhaps unique today in that *all* the words are known to the man-in-the-street:

> Any old iron, any old iron, any-any-any old iron:
> You look sweet, you do look a treat,
> You look dapper from your napper to your feet . . .

Among his other songs were 'Henery the Eighth' and 'Boiled Beef and Carrots', and so identified with East End mythology was Champion that working men's eating-houses advertised 'A Harry Champion, 1s', knowing that the message would get through.

To many of the audiences, Tom Costello (1863–1943) was a one-song man, 'Comrades', a heart-on-the-sleeve speciality, though his 'At Trinity Church I Met My Doom' had considerably more bite. Costello cultivated the fashion for patriotic songs brought about by the Boer War. These included 'Good-bye,

Dolly Gray', 'Soldiers of the Queen', and 'The Absent-minded Beggar', irreproachable sentiment matched with insipid tunes, a cynical package for the gallery.

Leo Dryden (1863–1939) had a speciality song, too, 'The Miner's Dream of Home', and one cannot imagine a performer with such a small range being a success in any other sphere than music hall. There were other performers who wore better because they did other things than merely stand up and sing a dolorous song. Songs were only a small part of the act of Little Tich (Harry Relph), who made his debut at the Rosherville Gardens in 1880, and was noted for his impersonations and his big flapping boots. His knockabout style anticipated the antics of early film comics. Mark Sheridan (1867–1918) got laughs simply on account of the way he dressed, in long knee-length coat, creased and crumpled, and extravagantly flared trousers, but Sheridan also pumped a number of music-hall classics into the repertoire such as 'Who Were You With Last Night?' and 'I Do Like to Be Beside the Seaside'. He kept going throughout World War I, and his song 'Here We Are, Here We Are, Here We Are Again' proved an acceptable marching song, similar in vein if perhaps slightly better musically than 'Tipperary' (sung by Florrie Forde in the Isle of Man two years before the war broke out).

George Robey (1869–1954) was better than his material. He was the equivalent of the gentleman-ranker in the pragmatic and slightly sleazy world of the music hall. The son of a civil engineer, Robey started his career as the stooge of a stage hypnotist, but he rapidly made his mark as the purveyor of suggestive naughtiness. The songs that he delivered, such as 'I Stopped, I Looked, I Listened', were nothing without the dead-pan delivery, the pseudo-clerical attire, and the air of surprise when the innuendo was grasped by his audience. In tremendous demand, Robey would frequently do four theatres in a night, travelling around in his own brougham. A legend in his own lifetime, Robey did not leave a heritage of convivial song as his contemporary, Harry Lauder, did.

Lauder was at his peak during the Edwardian period, and was one of the few to reach the £1,000 a week mark (at the Pavilion, Glasgow). It is difficult to evaluate such a sum in present-day

Harry Lauder brought the comic Scotsman, 'I Love a Lassie' and 'Roamin' in the Gloamin'' to the Sassenach. (Strand)

currency, and it has been suggested by economists that one should multiply by ten to get a viable equivalent. Thus Scottish *kitsch* was rewarded by immense sums of money, though it is debatable whether the world is a brighter place for 'I Love a Lassie' (1905) and 'Roamin' in the Gloamin'' (1910), both of them inserted into Glasgow pantomimes. Lauder is a rare example of a performer making his mark outside London, and of a regional idiom making a national impact. The Lauder songs were of a kind that devalued music-hall song—undemanding and self-indulgent. Lauder was also arch ('Stop Yer Ticklin' Jock') and pulled out all the stops for 'Keep Right on to the End of the Road'. He paid great attention to, as he put it, 'playing on the heartstrings of men and women' and he was the answer to a theatre manager's dream. Lauder did not have to knock himself out, like Little Tich, or develop a subtle *rapport* with his audience, like Robey, or even possess the professionalism of Harry Champion. He just had to stand on the stage in his kilt and trot out his set-pieces.

Song was not much of a feature of the stage act of Harry Tate (1873–1940), renowned for his situation comedy. George Robey had his eyebrows, Tate had his false moustache. He can be seen as a television performer ahead of his time, and his sketches dealing with motoring, fishing, billiards, and golfing filled a gap between burlesque and the stand-up comic. Nevertheless he did leave one of the best of the World War I tunes, 'Good-byee',

and one of the eternal catchphrases, 'How's Your Father?'
(invariably answered, 'All Right!').

Many of the stars travelled to America to appear in vaudeville,
and one of those who could earn twice as much in the United
States as in Britain was Wilkie Bard, somewhat surprisingly, as
there is little doubt that he lacked the charisma of his more
famous contemporaries. He was very good at character parts,
and had a sharp eye for contemporary events, using them as
pegs for songs. The suffragette movement evoked 'Put Me on
an Island Where the Girls Are Few', and he was in strong demand
for the tongue-twister 'She Sells Seashells on the Seashore'. Billy
Merson (1881–1947) was a run-of-the-mill comedian until 1914
when he brought out 'The Spaniard That Blighted My Life', a
quickfire humorous song that was taken up by a number of
between-the-wars artistes.

G. H. Elliott did not die until 1962 and was thus involved in
the trendy music-hall revival. First appearing in 1902, he eventually realised that his metier was black-faced work, and took
over the mantle of Stratton. Perhaps his best-known song was
'Sue, Sue, Sue, I'm Very Much in Love with You'. Will Fyffe,
although born in 1885, did not break into the London music-
hall scene until 1921. There were a number of singers who were
known for just one song—George Bastow (1872–1914) with
'The Galloping Major', Charles Whittle for 'Let's All Go Down
the Strand', and Harry Fragson with 'Hullo, Who's Your Lady
Friend?'

Many of the singers were merely vehicles for their songs, so
many puppets to be pushed on to the stage and do their piece for
an audience that asked only to be tendered the familiar. The
women stars have a good deal more individuality, and performers such as Kate Carney worked themselves into their roles.
Marie Kendall produced a winner with 'Just Like the Ivy' in
1902, but she was eclipsed by Vesta Victoria and Florrie Ford.
Vesta Victoria (née Lawrence) caught the audience's fancy with
'Daddy Wouldn't Buy Me a Bow-Wow' and later the mock-
tragic 'Waiting at the Church'. But like Florrie Forde she did not
let the pathos get out of hand, and behind the sentiment there was
a vein of astringency.

The songs made famous by Florrie Forde (1874–1941) read like a roll-call of music-hall hits: 'Down at the Old Bull and Bush', 'Oh, oh, Antonio', 'Has Anybody Here Seen Kelly?', 'Hold Your Hand Out, Naughty Boy', and 'She's a Lassie From Lancashire'. She lived somewhat in the shadow of Marie Lloyd, and although she had her own share of exuberance she found it difficult to match the legend.

The most electrifying of the ladies was, however, Lottie Collins, who created a furore when she sang 'Ta-ra-ra-boom-de-ay' at the Tivoli in 1891, leading to a fifteen-minutes-a-night spot at the Gaiety netting her £150 a week. In a big Gainsborough hat and short red frock, revealing a froth of white petticoat, Lottie Collins brought Parisian daring to the London halls. She wore herself out singing and dancing this song, but it was taken over by other spritely music-hall soubrettes who did not wish to enter into a purely singing duel with the gently aging greats.

Other music-hall ladies avoided competition by dressing in reversed drag. The male impersonators were precursors of pantomime principal boys and the polar opposite of panto-mime dames. Perhaps the best was Vesta Tilley (1864–1952) who was so much the rage in the nineties that she set men's fashions. Miss Tilley wore well, and was in the £300 a week class when she was in her fifties, still relying on the curious sexual ambiguity of a pretty woman simulating a man. A verse from one of her hits epitomises the type of song she made fashionable:

He's very well-known is Algy, to the ladies on the stage;
Such a jolly good chap is Algy, just now he's all the rage.
Such a jolly big favourite, Algy ,with the barmaids at the 'Cri'.
He's very well-known is Algy,
As the Piccadilly Johnny with the little glass eye.

Nevertheless, the classic transvestite ditty was not hers, but Ella Shields's—'I'm Burlington Bertie from Bow'. Ella Shields was born in 1879, and like Vesta Tilley made the Edwardian hermaphrodite, the knut, an acceptable social figure.

The immense popularity of these men and women, whose names

Vesta Tilley (1864-1952) was perhaps the leading male impersonator of the age.

and songs were known throughout the length and breadth of the kingdom, their features immortalised on picture postcards and sheet-music covers, were both the saving and the ruin of the music hall. The music-hall managers could not afford to do without the stars, but they soaked up enormous salaries. The audiences, seemingly, would have liked their favourites to go on singing until they dropped, but without fresh blood and a new repertoire an entertainment industry stagnates. Marie Kendall reckoned that she sang 'Just Like the Ivy' more than 5,000 times on the stage.

With high rentals, high salaries and high running expenses, music-hall management played safe, and newcomers to the trade were obliged to adopt the tried and tested favourites when their originators had either died, gone into some other field such as musical comedy or revue, or were past it. Lottie Collins died in 1910, but had she lived longer the frantic exertions needed for 'Ta-ra-ra-boom-de-ay' would have eventually proved too much for her.

American salary scales encouraged many performers to try their hand there, and managers, panic-stricken by the prospect of having to try newcomers, were obliged to match these scales. At the close of the Edwardian period Harry Lauder was demanding a minimum of £500 a week, and even then the theatre and the management had to suit him. He was offered £800 a week by the Empire and turned it down. By dying in 1904 Dan Leno missed the really big pickings, and it is doubtful whether he topped the £300 mark. Marie Lloyd was in the £240 a week class, and Little Tich commanded £500 a week. Nevertheless, it must not be supposed that managers were mad to pay such salaries—in straight theatre Henry Irving was making as much as this, and more.

Even relatively minor figures such as Eugene Stratton and

A night scene in Leicester Square with the Empire in the background.

Dan Leno died in 1904 *and was therefore too late to capitalise on the golden age of the music hall.*

R. G. Knowles were in the £200 a week class, though in the nineties the newly-established Albert Chevalier was content to work three turns nightly for £36.

Nor was it only in the West End that management was put on the rack. Provincial favourites of little account except that audiences had taken to them were regularly marking up £100 a week (£50,000 a year in today's money, and with minimal tax). Not surprisingly, managers were obliged to spend a part of their day brushing off enthusiastic comics and singers who wanted to turn professional. In an interview in 1909, Alfred Butt, the manager of the Palace Theatre of Varieties, pointed out his difficulties. Responsible for the booking of between two and three hundred turns a year, he looked askance at the idea that he never saw newcomers.

I rarely refuse to hear or see anything or anybody. People who tell you it is impossible to get a hearing in London don't know what they are talking about. I'm just as anxious to see them as they are to come, but it is dreary work. Still, there is always the hope of something fresh, always the fear that the thing you might decline to see is good, and may get snapped up by someone else and become a big hit.

There were some whom Butt drew the line at. The suburban lady with a hyphenated name who had sung at an 'At Home' and whose friends had suggested, sarcastically, that she went on the stage:

If I say I will hear her she will come and warble 'Dear Heart!' (it's always 'Dear Heart!') in an indifferent drawing-room voice, and seems bewildered at the lack of enthusiasm. She will leave with an expression of resignation or indignation.

Naturally singers and comedians could not fill a music-hall programme by themselves, and there were all kinds of subsidiary acts, from the top ballet dancers earning £250 a week (with Pavlova on £750) down to the conjurors and the acrobats. Miss Emmiline Ethardo in her Ménage Artistique, Lieutenant Frank Travis, the Society Ventriloquist, Frank Mayo and Company in the Realistic Cowboy Sketch 'The Bargain', The Four Richardinis, Sensational Gymnasts, the Charmoniane, Refined Musical Novelty, not to mention the Bioscope operator, all had their parts to play, surrounding the stars like acolytes or offering solace when the person at the top of the bill had not come up to expectations. The Professors of Legerdemain and The Fletchers (in their great Laughable Skating Act) were often treated as part of the background, interludes while the singer regained breath, content with a living wage and philosophical about their future when hands lost their cunning, legs were not so agile, and reaching for ropes and trapeze bars was like reaching for the moon. Unsung, unheralded, they have dropped into the gloom unlit by posthumous candles.

It took all sorts to fill a music-hall stage from Pavlova at £750 a week, through conjurors and acrobats, down to the back line of the chorus, fair game for the 'knuts' and the stage-door johnnies. (Woman's World)

Edwardian music hall offered comfortable jobs for large numbers of musicians, especially in the provinces where there was little alternative employment. Some of the orchestras were of a very high standard (at one time it was said that the Alhambra orchestra was second only to that of Covent Garden), not at all like the wheezing incompetent bands that one can remember in the orchestra pits of between-the-wars music halls. The Palace had a first-rate leader of the orchestra from 1896 in Herman Finck, who became musical director in 1909, retaining the job until 1921. Finck was also an excellent composer of light music and especially revues—*The Passing Show* (1914) was his. The entertainment form that eclipsed the music hall—the cinema—did not offer quite the same scope to orchestral players, though pianists were more fortunate than most.

Edwardian music halls kept their audiences because there was nothing comparable offered to them, though the vogue for musical comedy hived off the wealthier patrons. The more talented performers succeeded in perpetuating the *rapport* between stage and auditorium that had existed in the smaller Victorian halls and the 'free and easies', persuading the audience that they were at one with them. Had the supply of memorable and tuneful songs dried up, music hall would have felt the wind of change considerably earlier, but somehow this never happened. The backroom boys, the song and lyric writers, their names unknown except to the performers (and sometimes not even then), kept going, though most of them have joined the limbo of impressionists and acrobats.

Many of the performers prided themselves on writing their own material. Harry Lauder certainly did (with help), Mark Sheridan claimed that he did, but there are others lost in the footnotes of musical history—Edgar Bateman and George le Brunn ('It's a Great Big Shame'), Felix McGlennon ('Comrades'), Harry Bedford and Terry Sullivan ('Bit of a Ruin That Cromwell Knocked about a Bit'). Some of them made substantial sums, while others were conned into parting with the rights for a few pounds. As with music-hall success, it was a lottery, with the winning ticket going to the big battalions.

The Drury Lane theatre, noted for its pantomimes, a refuge for music-hall artists who were in danger of being overlooked. (Around London)

CHAPTER THREE

THE SHOP BALLAD

WHEREAS MUSIC HALL harked back to the song and supper rooms and saloons of the early nineteenth century and musical comedy went back to burlesque, the ballad concert was of comparatively recent origin. It was evolved by publishers of music as a way to put their music before the public, and the two leading practitioners were the firms of Boosey, first in the field in the spring of 1867, and Chappell.

All the songs and concerted pieces in that first concert were British, and they included genuine folk songs, pseudo-folk songs, good old standbys like 'Home, Sweet Home', a 1612 madrigal by Gibbons, and, far outnumbering all the others put together, modern songs of an undemanding nature, usually dealing with love, God or nature. In the 1920s a critic said that the test of a bad song was whether it had God in the last line. Be that as it may, the rapturous reception given to the artistes made certain that such works as 'When Shall We Two Meet Again?' by Glover, 'Strangers Yet' by Claribel, and 'Give' by Sullivan were destined to be in the repertoire for a long time to come, though the epitome of ballad perfection, 'The Lost Chord', had to wait until 1877 (though, for the publishers, it was worth waiting for, as it sold 500,000 copies).

Publishers who managed to reach the ballad audience were sure of rich rewards. This audience was not necessarily in the concert hall to hear such artistes as Mme Sainton-Dolby singing 'The

The variety of ballads produced by Chappell & Co can be gauged by this advertisement.

Playing 'The Rosary' with one finger

Angels' Home' (by Sainton-Dolby) or Mme Lemmens Sherring-ton doing one of Moore's Irish melodies. The buyers of the music, customarily retailing at four shillings (a day's pay for the working man), were the drawing-room amateurs who read enthusiastic reports of the new ballads in the weekly press, or had heard of fetching and lachrymose songs through the middle-class grape-vine operating at musical evenings and 'at homes'.

The replacement on the throne of Queen Victoria by her son Edward did not mean any diminution in the popularity of the ballad. Those most captivated by the sentiments enshrined therein were those least affected by the wave of permissiveness that had swept through the nineties, were more than ever censorious of the music hall, and were not in the opera-going class.

Notwithstanding all the technological progress that had been made during the second half of the nineteenth century, it remained certain that if a family wanted music in the home they would almost certainly have to play it themselves. The cylinder musical box with its small repertoire and tinkling sound was no real substitute, and the tone of the disc musical boxes, though they were now modestly priced and were no bigger than a hat-box, was wearisome and reminded the genteel too much of the jangling street pianos that kept the poor *au fait* with the current 'top twenty'. At the start of the twentieth century the gramophone was a wheezing, pathetic instrument that parodied music, and the Pianola, good as it was, was fairly expensive and had to be rolled on to an already existing piano. There was nothing that counterfeited with anything like accuracy the human voice; and the song was considered to be the prime expression of human emotion.

The publishers, knowing that this captive public existed in colossal numbers, not only laid out great sums of money on promoting their songs, but even built their own halls at which their ballads would be sung, and where the response of an audience would be weighed up. They also hired those halls built by piano manufacturers such as the Steinway Hall in Lower Seymour Street.

There had been some changes in the make-up of ballad programmes between 1867 and 1901. One of the ballad singers, Antoinette Sterling, had become enamoured of the songs of Schubert and Schumann, and had gradually introduced these into her programmes, and the occasional aria from Italian opera was sung. These were tolerated rather than welcomed by the ballad concertgoer.

Many singers built up huge reputations by their work in ballads. In 1868 Mme Patey-Whyttock—hyphenated ladies gave class to the proceedings—made herself a secure niche with 'Kathleen Mavourneen'. She kept going until 1894 when, after singing 'The Banks of Allan Water' with its ominous concluding line 'There a corse lay she', she collapsed and died soon afterwards. In 1870 Sims Reeves and Charles Santley, two of the most important Victorian singers, made their first appearances at ballad concerts. Neither found anything humiliating in dashing off ballads, though Santley was scathing about the genre in his autobiography ('imbecile trash'). Among his favourites were such curios as 'The Yeoman's Wedding' by Prince Poniatowski, 'Father O'Flynn' by Sir Charles Villiers Stanford, and 'Simon the Cellarer'.

Sims Reeves became famous for the times he did not sing as much as for the times he did sing. He admits that he had lost in earnings £100,000 by what he termed 'over-scrupulousness' (others said he was drunk) and his anxiety to be at his best. He was also notorious for his 'farewell' concerts, which lasted twelve years.

> He passed away in 1900, being at the time over eighty years old, only a few months after he had given a 'Farewell' tour in the provinces, which lasted upwards of twelve weeks. With that tour he created a melancholy record, for, owing a good deal to the enfeebled state of his health, he did not appear at a single one of his concerts. At some of the places the reading of the telegram announcing his inability to sing evoked such scenes of fury as will never be forgotten by any of the artistes who had to fill out the programme.

Ballad concerts were not all sweetness and light.

The Edwardian ballad singers had the advantage of a vast stock of sure-fire winners, and many of the singers and songs had been in on the ballad scene since the outset. A ballad singer did not have to change with the times, and no matter what state of decrepitude he or she was in, if the sentiment (which, all admitted, was more important than the music) could be put over, a welcome was assured.

A singer-composer whose work was appreciated by the Edwardians as much as by the Victorians was Michael Maybrick, better known under his pseudonym Stephen Adams. Many of his songs are still sung today, especially those with religious connotations. He wrote 'Nancy Lee', 'The Midshipmite', 'The Star of Bethlehem', 'The Holy City', 'They All Love Jack', and

A drawing-room song escaped from its proper environment.
(Punch)

SONGS AND THEIR SINGERS

" Yew harxed me woy hoi larved when larve should be
A thing hun-der-eamed hof larve twixt yew han me.
Yew moight hin-tereat the sun tew cease tew she-oine
Has seek tew sty saw deep a larve has moine."

'Nirvana'. Another long-server was Edward Lloyd. His name was linked with 'Down the Vale', 'The Last Watch', and, still a drawing-room song to be conjured with, 'I'll Sing Thee Songs of Araby'. Antoinette Sterling, much as she liked the songs of Schubert and Schumann, was noted for 'The Lost Chord'—described by E. F. Benson as a test-piece for tears on which singers tried their strength—'Love's Old Sweet Song', and 'Darby and Joan'. Miss Sterling was one of Mr Arthur Boosey's properties, and in 1908 he declared that he could recall no vocalist whose songs had had such a persistently large sale over so long a period.

What constituted a suitable song for an Edwardian ballad concert?

There were first of all folk songs and sea songs, or art music masquerading in those guises. Charles Dibdin (1745–1814) wrote many of the sea-songs fondly believed to be Olde Englyshe, such as 'Ben Backstay', 'The Lass That Loves a Sailor', and 'Tom Bowling', while James Hook (1746–1827) created a multi-purpose song, suitable for all occasions, in 'The Lass of Richmond Hill'. Traditional Scottish tunes had long enjoyed wide circulation in England, and were collected by the curious when the wealth of English folk song was ignored: there was no shortage of hacks to fit words to them. One of the songs featured in Boosey's first ballad concert was 'My Heart Is Sair for Somebody' with the succinct programme note, 'Scotch'. Irish tunes were also popular. Between 1808 and 1834 Thomas Moore wrote a long series of *Irish Melodies*, and the composers John Stevenson (1761-1833) and Henry Bishop (1786–1855) put music to them. The result, eminently singable and widely looked upon as genuinely old songs, was a succession including 'The Minstrel Boy' and 'The Harp That Once Through Tara's Halls'.

The most famous of Irish traditional tunes was, and is, 'The Londonderry Air', published in a collection of ancient music in 1855 and picked up years later by the lawyer/ballad writer, Fred Weatherly, who made 'Danny Boy' out of it:

> Oh, Danny boy, the pipes, the pipes are calling
>   From glen to glen, and down the mountain side.
> The summer's gone, and all the roses falling (for-orl-ling)
>   It's you, it's you must go and I must bide.

Unquestionably Weatherly did not realise how much he has to answer for, and one sometimes wishes that a lyric writer who had beaten Weatherly to the punch and had written two sets of words to the same melody—Alfred Percival Graves with 'Emer's Farewell' and 'Erin's Apple-Blossom'—had had more fortune. Moore—who, to do him justice, was Irish—was also a composer on his own account, and the music and the words of another drawing-room ballad with an all-round appeal that must vie with 'Home Sweet Home', 'The Last Rose of Summer', were his. This air was borrowed by Flotow for his opera *Martha* (1847) (and was also used by the eccentric composer of the twenties, Lord Berners, to hang a parody on).

Somewhat fortuitously, Haydn appears frequently in Victorian and Edwardian ballad concert programmes, though he is often spelled Haydon. Haydn wrote fourteen original song-settings of English words that were unpretentious and graceful, though the 'Sailor's Song' is marred because Haydn thought that hurly-burly was an equivalent of fa-la-la, a useful device to slip in anywhere.

C. E. Horn (1786–1849) was responsible for another popular ballad, 'Cherry Ripe', and J. L. Hatton was the composer of the Santley favourite, 'Simon the Cellarer'. In this, Hatton was going back to the old definition of ballad as a piece that tells a story. Balfe had a good deal of success with 'I Shot an Arrow in the Air', and he did a version of 'The Village Blacksmith', but his was not the one that captivated the cognoscenti: that was written by a singer, W. H. Weiss (1820–67). J. P. Knight's 'She Wore a Wreath of Roses' was not so popular among the Edwardians as it was among the Victorians, though Hullah's 'Three Fishers' to words by Charles Kingsley went on and on, and no doubt still does. After its introduction at a ballad concert, 'there was a tumult of applause: people rose in their places and cheered, waving hats and handkerchiefs in their excitement'.

Hadyn songs, somewhat surprisingly, were very popular among Victorian and Edwardian ballad-concert audiences.
(Punch)

These composers were all dead by the Edwardian period, and no doubt the considerable royalties were making widows, sons and daughters glad that the song-writers had not stuck to serious music. For there was great wealth to be made from a single song. A few minutes spent jotting down a heart-easing ballad could set a composer up for life, and it was not surprising that serious composers turned their attentions to these money-making possibilities, or that they were on the defensive about these little indiscretions. It is, indeed, difficult to find composers who did not commit infidelity to their muses.

Hubert Parry (1848–1918), with four symphonies and three oratorios to his name plus a drawing-room ballad that became a second national anthem ('Jerusalem'), wrote 'When Lovers Meet Again', weak by even ballad standards: Charles Villiers Stanford's 'Father O'Flynn' was a favourite piece of blarney; Sir Frederick Cowen was more prolific, and rang up more than 300 songs (as well as four operas, six symphonies, and more than a dozen cantatas). In his sober old age in the 1920s, Cowen felt that he had to explain himself in an article 'Then—and Now' in a kind of encyclopedia-in-parts, *Musical Masterpieces*:

> The sentimental ballad of my own early days was, of course, a type of its own, and there are people nowadays who profess to be astonished that it could be so popular. But *autres temps, autres moeurs*. At that period, serious music yielded very little money, and we musicians had to live. All the same, some seventy or eighty of my songs were on serious lines, and many of them, such as 'Onaway, Awake', 'A Birthday', and 'At the Mid Hour of Night', are still constantly being sung.

Cowen stated that the most popular of his ballads was 'The Better Land' and he wondered whether it was a misfortune rather than otherwise, for it had haunted him ever since. At a birthday party, George Grossmith had sprung a surprise on Cowen by singing a parody of it:

I hear thee speak of a Better Land,

Written by young Freddy Cowen's hand,
Mother, where did he get that tune?
Where did he steal it, oh, tell me soon?
Did it come from Handel's grand 'Messiah'?
Or Charlie Gounod's 'Ave Maria'?
Not there, not there, my child.

Arthur Jacobs in *A History of Song* (1960) wrote that we need not blame the Cowens, the Parrys, and the Stanfords for accepting the temptation to make money quickly from the craftsmanlike application of ready-made formulas, any more than one blames a mid-twentieth-century composer for writing film music. Jacobs praises certain of Cowen's songs for their 'real individuality and shapeliness'.

There were composers for the Edwardian ballad market who found their métier in this undemanding genre, such as Liza Lehmann (1862–1918) who had much success with her 'In a Persian Market', based on the *Rubaiyat* of Omar Khayyam, that somewhat precious piece of Turkish delight for suburban aesthetes and amply matched by the music. Although written originally for four voices and piano, 'In a Persian Market', was rapidly served up in a more convenient form. Miss Lehmann, in private life Mrs Herbert Bedford and finding a place in *Who's Who*, was herself a concert singer from 1885 to 1894.

Ballad writing was a respectable occupation, especially when the ballad savoured of something superior. 'In a Persian Market' was pop music masquerading as serious work, and much of the success of the ballad was due to the belief of listeners that they were being improved, and their relief that 'good' music was not such hard going after all. The Edwardian ballad as practised by Liza Lehmann was the equivalent of a 'coffee-table' book—lush, easy to pick up and put down, and not demanding too much expenditure of attention. The true colours of Liza Lehmann show not in the entries in *Who's Who*—the musical farce *Sergeant Brue*, settings of Longfellow, Tennyson's *In Memoriam* and *The Golden Threshold* ('an Indian song-garland')—but in the basics of pounds and pence in Chappell & Co's 1912 catalogue of the 'latest song and ballad successes' which lists Miss Lehmann's

'Daddy's Sweetheart', 'Little Moccasins', 'Clementina's Song', and 'Thoughts Have Wings'.

'In a Persian Market' had its detractors. The producer of the musical farce *Sergeant Brue* stipulated firmly that there were to be 'No "Persian Gardens" here!' and Miss Lehmann was told by a woman friend, enthusiastic after listening to 'In a Persian Garden', that she 'thought she was at Liberty's'. Liberty's was the famous West End store that started the British vogue for artistic furniture and decor. Even Miss Lehmann thought this compliment double-edged.

Perhaps Miss Lehmann's most humiliating experience was during the performance of her *The Vicar of Wakefield*. The adaptation of the Oliver Goldsmith novel was made by Laurence Housman, who laughed so much during the performance that he was thrown out of the theatre by the manager, George Curzon, and thereafter refused to have his name associated with the work.

It is interesting to note that women composers were as much in evidence in Edwardian drawing-room music as they had been in the Victorian ballad. Another prolific lady composer was Maude Valérie White (1855–1937), and being a few years older than Liza Lehmann she enjoys the cachet of being the first woman composer to become established in England (the older Victorians had been amateurs without musical training). Born in Dieppe, Miss White entered the Royal Acacemy of Music in 1876 and studied composition under Macfarren. A portion of a Mass was performed by the students of the Royal Academy. Ill-health encouraged her to live in South America for a while, but she settled in London in 1883.

Her best-known song was 'The Devout Lover', and she was adept at setting Herrick and Shelley to music. The words of Robert Browning caused her more trouble, but, an admirable professional, she coped well and was by no means a drawing-room hack such as the Victorian Claribel and the Edwardian Florence Aylward. Sir Arthur Somervell (1863–1937) provided some drawing-room ballads, and was one of the first to seize upon the gentle melancholy of A. E. Housman's *A Shropshire Lad*. Elgar entered the ballad stakes, and no doubt the publishers held great hopes of a man who could strike the public ear with the 'Pomp

and Circumstance' marches, 'Salut d'amour', 'Chanson de matin'
and 'Chanson de nuit', which were said by Frank Howes to
coexist embarrassingly alongside his great works. But Elgar's
drawing-room ballads were not even significant enough to
coexist, and were soon forgotten.

In 1908 a number of ballad composers were asked which were
their most popular songs. Most of them avowed that the public
choice was not theirs. Florence Aylward declared that the public
showed a preference for her 'Beloved, It Is Morn', with 'Love's
Coronation' running it close. The style she preferred was 'the
quiet, graceful, dreamy, melodious song, with a slight touch of
melancholy', though she thought, as Cowen put it in his apologia,
autres temps autres moeurs, and she might soon incline to an
ardent love-song. Teresa del Riego had no doubt that 'Oh, Dry
Those Tears' was her most popular song, and averred 'while I was
writing it I felt it would appeal to the public, for something told
me that it was the truth. I think that the qualities most essential
to success in composing songs are truth of expression, and
harmony, combined with originality.' Miss del Riego was letting
her fine feelings run away with her, and the originality of her
songs can be assessed by the titles that Chappell was promoting:
'Little Brown Bird', 'Your Picture', 'Hayfields and Butterflies',
'The Red Rose Wooed the White Rose', 'I Lay My Laurels
at Your Feet', and 'Your Heart Is a Haven'.

Miss Frances Allitsen, like Miss White, had had an academic
training, studying at the Guildhall School of Music, and had a
piano sonata (1881) and two concert overtures (1884) to her
credit, plus more than 100 songs and duets, the most popular of
which was 'Prince Ivan's Song', to words by Marie Corelli.
This song, said Miss Corelli, was 'the very fire of sound'. Noel
Johnson reckoned that his lugubrious 'If Thou Wert Blind'
was a public favourite, admitting that both he and his publisher
were amazed when it sold nearly 100,000 copies.

Hamish McCunn showed some embarrassment at being
included amongst this band of best-sellers, for great hopes had
been entertained of his being the leader of a new school of
Scottish composers on the strength of his overture (though he
called it an orchestral symphony) *Land of the Mountain and the*

Flood, written when he was nineteen, and his opera *Jeanie Deans*, based on Walter Scott's *The Heart of Midlothian*, which posterity has seen as watered-down Verdi (though it was revived in Glasgow in 1951 for the Festival of Britain). McCunn (1868–1916) was defensive about the popularity of his song 'Two Eyes': 'In all I have published over 100 songs, but they are mostly of what I should call the "chamber music" or "cabinet-picture" class, which rarely appeal to the masses as greatly as does a song such as "Two Eyes" or compositions of the ballad concert order'.

Hermann Löhr did not share McCunn's contempt for the public, and deferentially commented: 'A number of my humble efforts have, I am proud to say, attained a considerable degree of success'. This was an underestimate, for whereas most of the songs of his contemporaries have long since disappeared, Löhr's 'Little Grey Home in the West' and 'Where My Caravan Has Rested' have remained in the repertoire, proof, if proof be needed, that the Edwardian ballad is not dead. Löhr did not mind his works being called 'shop ballads'; he was carrying on the family trade (his father was also a ballad composer).

A perfect example of the professional musician dropping his standards to cash in on the vogue for ballads is furnished by the career of Luigi Denza, composer of the brainless 'Funicula-Funiculi' which has all the scrubbing-board monotony of the worst music-hall patter-song. Denza, born in 1846, proud to proclaim himself 'Chevalier de l'ordre de la Couronne d'Italie' was a director of the London Academy of Music, a professor of singing at the Royal Academy of Music, and composer of an opera staged in Naples in 1876. He settled in London in 1883, and between his multifarious activities he found time to write 600 songs, the consecutive titles of which sound like the plot of a musical comedy, 'Come to Me', 'Call Me Back', 'Fettered'.

Sims Reeves and Charles Santley were only two of the top singers who found huge financial rewards in singing ballads. Not only would the big names receive the usual fee for their concerts, but on top of this they would receive a royalty from the ballad publishers for plugging their songs, which were often called 'royalty ballads' as well as shop ballads. Lord Ernest

Hamilton gives an interesting example of the impact of the operatic star Melba singing at the private house of his brother, the Duke of Abercorn:

> Melba entertained us for quite a while and at last, as a *finale*, broke into the 'Banks of Allan Water'. She sang through all three verses and, as she finished, we became aware of strange gurgling sounds coming from the direction of the Black Library. One of the party in some alarm ran to the door and flung it open, whereupon we discovered to our amazement that in the Black Library was assembled, as an invisible audience, the whole of the domestic staff, all the female members of which were sobbing convulsively. The last verse of 'Allan Water' had broken them down. What higher tribute could possibly be paid to the sympathetic quality of a singer's voice?

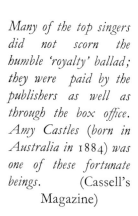

Many of the top singers did not scorn the humble 'royalty' ballad; they were paid by the publishers as well as through the box office. Amy Castles (born in Australia in 1884) was one of these fortunate beings. (Cassell's Magazine)

Did a voice have anything to do with it? In 1907 an opera singer who doubled as a balladmonger (selling and singing in this context can hardly be separated), Lillian Nordica, wrote on the technique of singing ballads, mentioning in passing that 'the sentiment of a ballad is of almost more importance than the music' and that 'the text is the most important thing'. She considered that enunciation took precedence over hitting a high note, and that a singer should remember, 'I know the words, but my public does not know the words and I am telling them something that I want each one's individual interest in.'

Miss Nordica complained that the simplest words are mispronounced in singing, and poured scorn on the young lady who sang about the 'pratty, pratty warbling choir', decreed that 'wind' should always be sung with a long 'i', irrespective of the demands of common sense, and considered that publishers often erred. She recalled an occasion when she was singing a religious piece and 'Oh-Gee' appeared at the end of one page with 'rusalem' on the following.

Like music-hall celebrities, the stars of the ballad concert had their specialities. Clara Butt was associated with 'Abide With Me', and by thus giving it secular connections she made it a feature of the football Cup Final. Clara Butt was born in 1873 and married the singer Kennerley Rumford in 1900, having made her debut as a contralto at the Lyceum Theatre in 1892 before the Prince of Wales (later Edward VII). She was one of the first singers of 'Land of Hope and Glory', and also made a feature in her programmes of 'Softly Awakes My Heart' from Saint-Saëns' *Samson and Delilah*. The British public took Clara Butt to its capacious heart just as it had the ballet dancer Taglioni more than half a century earlier. The model for his Trilby, Miss Butt, declared du Maurier,

> was so tender, so humble, so touchingly simple and sweet that one melted at the sight of her. No such magnificent or seductive apparition has ever been seen before or since on any stage or platform. Her voice was so immense in its softness, richness, freshness, that it seemed to be pouring itself out from all round: one felt it to be not only faultless,

Dame Clara Butt and her singer husband Mr Rumford were sufficiently well-known to be 'postcard celebrities'.

but infallible: and the seduction, the novelty of it, the strangely sympathetic quality!

The *Era* was equally impressed:

> She may be described in the words of Lord Tennyson, as 'a daughter of the gods, divinely tall', for she is six feet two in height, though only nineteen years of age. Her voice is a contralto of the purest quality . . . rich, sympathetic, and equal throughout its entire range.

Queen Victoria's approval set the seal on public adoration. 'I have never liked the English language before,' she said, 'but in your mouth it is beautiful'. Clara Butt could do no wrong: she was offered St Paul's Cathedral to be married in, but preferred her humble Bristol. In 1926, looking back, she declared: 'I have sung many hundreds of songs during my career, and I do not think I have sung any bad ones'. Naive or contentious, no one could argue with Dame Clara Butt. She was an institution.

'Softly Awakes My Heart' was also the favourite song of Edna Thornton, coupled with a number from Verdi's *A Masked Ball*. Ada Crossley had made her first London appearance in 1895, and although she sang five times for Queen Victoria, who said that she had a beautiful voice and was a true artist, she reached her peak during the Edwardian period, making a speciality of the spaghetti-Italian 'Caro Mio Ben'. The favourite song of Agnes Nicholls, who was in great demand for the oratorio circuit, speeding between Birmingham, Gloucester, Norwich, Preston, Hereford and Leeds, was 'Robin Adair'. Louise Kirkby Lunn had made her operatic debut in 1908 with *Shamus O'Brien*, but made her main impact in ballad concert with Hullah's 'Three Fishers Went Sailing'. Miss Gleeson-White as a young girl caught the ear of Elgar, who selected her to appear in his *Caractacus*, but as a ballad singer her favourite song was 'Bredon Hill', Housman's words served up with unexceptional music by Dalhousie Young.

Many of these young ladies went on the defensive over their plundering raids into royalty ballad, but Ella Russell (Covent Garden debut 1886) breezily laid about her when it was suggested that she was perhaps devaluing her talent by singing that old pot-boiler 'Il Bacio' (The Dove):

> It is such a delightful song, and so cheerful and melodious that the very thought of it raises one's spirits! And besides, the public like it so! You may say what you like, but a singer must get more satisfaction out of singing a song that the public really appreciate. When the opening bars of 'Il Bacio' are struck up the audience invariably start to clap, and this puts one in a good humour right away.

The effort to invest ballads with artistic importance could be taken to ridiculous lengths, and in defending Antoinette Sterling from the charge of being 'a sublimated street singer' Fred Weatherly overstated the case with such assurance that one feels he was defending his own ballads by proxy:

> When she had words in which she really believed, such as 'Caller Herrin'', 'The Better Land' [words by the egregious Mrs Hemans], 'The Lost Chord', 'Darby and Joan' [which Weatherly himself wrote] and 'The Chorister' [music by

Sullivan, words by the ineffable Weatherly], she sang as one inspired by a mission. She was a divine revealer. She was not acting a part. She was herself and that self spoke to millions and stirred their hearts.

It is difficult to believe that the words of the pop ballads could inspire any mission, and it is worth-while to look at the opening lyrics to see what precisely the public was being subjected to:

Fair is my love!
So fair is he,
For him I live,
For him I sigh.
Hope still shall reign
Where'er I rove,
No time can change
My constant love.
 'Caro Mio Ben' (Fair Is My Love)

Three fishers went sailing out into the west,
Out into the west as the sun went down:
Each thought on the woman who lov'd him the best,
And the children stood watching them out of the town.
 'Three Fishers'

Breezes, lightly blowing,
Bear a message to my only dear!
When you meet him, softly greet him
From the one who lingers here!
 'Il Bacio' (The Dove)

Falling leaf and fading tree,
Lines of white in a sullen sea,
Shadows rising on you and me,
The swallows are making them ready to fly
Wheeling out on a windy sky,
Good-bye, summer, good-bye!
 'Good-bye'

The last song, the favourite of Alice Esty and countless others,

The First Time of Asking.

BY FREDERIC E. WEATHERLY.

"The first time of asking
 She blushed and hung her head,
She liked him as a—as a—friend,
 But nothing more," she said ;
She hoped he would forget her,
 And his heart he would not break,
And he might have the rose she wore,
 And keep it for her sake.

The second time of asking
 She was going far away,
They would not meet to-morrow,
 Or for many a long, long day ;
And he asked her if she loved him,
 And 'he said he loved her so,
But she sighed "she must be going,"
 And yet—she did not go !

The third time of asking
 She never spoke at all,
But softly in the starlight,
 He saw her teardrops fall ;
Then lifting up her eyes to his,
 She nestled to his breast,
For the love that is unspoken,
 Is the love that is the best !

Frederic E. Weatherly was one of the most prolific of lyric-writers, and 'The First Time of Asking' was typical of the products of his muse.
(Ludgate)

made the name of Signor Sir F. Paolo Tosti, KCVO, proof that a composer did not have to be an Elgar to get a knighthood (King Edward VII was very lavish in dispensing honours to the providers of the humdrum), and it is instructive to look at his songs to see what the acceptability level was—'Come to My Heart', 'For Ever and Ever', 'That Day', 'Let It Be Soon', 'Ask Me No More', 'Help Me to Pray', 'Yesterday', 'At the Convent Gate', and 'We Have Loved'. Tosti had been accompanist at Court, and on the strength of this charged one shilling a minute for piano lessons.

It is not surprising that British composers who had discovered the merits of folk song and were anxious to place their own

There was a market for picture postcard publishers from ballads. The story line was illustrated and printed in a series of four or so.

THE VOLUNTEER ORGANIST (1)

The preacher in the village Church one Sunday morning said:
"Our organist is ill to-day, will someone play instead?"
An anxious look crept o'er the face of every person there,
As eagerly they watched to see who'd fill the vacant chair.
A man then staggered down the aisle whose clothes were old and torn,
How strange a drunkard seemed to me in Church on Sunday morn;
But as he touched the organ keys, without a single word,
The melody that followed was the sweetest ever heard.

WORDS BY KIND PERMISSION OF W. PAXTON. OXFORD STREET. LONDON

arrangements and assimilations before the public—Ralph Vaughan Williams, for example, with 'Linden Lea'—were in despair when they found out about the pernicious rubbish that they had to displace. There were intelligent singers, such as Gervase Elwes, who were enthusiastic about what the balladmongers called 'art' songs, but they were outnumbered by those who were quite happy with the better-paying and undemanding. John McCormack ('the English Caruso') made his name not with his operatic roles but with 'I Hear You Calling Me'. It is interesting that when Arthur Boosey was approached by the composer, Charles Marshall, and McCormack, his three questions were: Can other singers do it? Can a soprano sing it? Will it catch on with the public?

The ballad singers believed that they had lots of taste, but, sadly, most of it was bad. They put their foot in it with gorgeous aplomb. When Amy Castles (born in Australia in 1884) was interviewed in 1907 she said:

> Two questions are often put to me. What are my favourite songs? Who is my favourite composer? My great wish is to play Ophelie in Ambroise Thomas's *Hamlet*; Juliette, in *Romeo and Juliette* [*sic*]; and Manon. In these operas are to be found the songs I like best. But you will never guess who is my pet composer! I am quite up-to-date in my choice, for he was born only twenty-two years ago. He is Ethelbert, the American. In my opinion he has done more for music during his short lifetime than has any other modern musician...

Mr Ethelbert, where are you now? Were you Ethelbert Nevin (1862–1901)?

Edwardian drawing-room ballad was personalised. In order of importance came the singer, the words, and the music. This was also true of music hall. The singers rated themselves very highly,

Left: Ballad singers often rated themselves highly, and considered that they were doing the audience a favour by projecting beautiful thoughts. (Ludgate)

Opposite: Love, sorrow, friendship, nature and patriotism were all components of the popular ballad, and with the rewards at stake there were few singers who scorned them. (Strand)

THE SUMS INDICATED SHOW WHAT THESE SINGERS RECEIVE FOR EVERY MINUTE THEY SING.

1. Teofani; 2. Patti; 3. Tetrazzini; 4. Caruso; 5. Melba.

and considered that they were doing the audience a favour by projecting beautiful thoughts. As with musical comedy, an eye had to be kept on the American market, and although the American public would not warm to some of the home-spun efforts and had a keen sense of the ridiculous when a fat soprano sang 'I'd be a butterfly, born in a bower', it could be pacified by

English singers doing its own ballad classics, in particular the songs of Stephen Foster (1826–64).

These travelled very well, and 'The Old Folks at Home', 'Oh, Susanna', 'My Old Kentucky Home', and 'Massa's in de Cold, Cold Ground' were warmly received at English ballad concerts. Foster was summed up in 1904 by Rupert Hughes in words that could well apply to many a British composer: 'Foster at his best trembled on the razor-edge between the perfect simplicity of folk-song and the maudlin banality of street song'.

An undemanding audience gets the entertainment it deserves, especially if it is rich and the performers are subsidised. The devotees of ballad did not wish to have their imaginations stretched. They were happy with bog-English ('Oh, we came up from Somerset/To see the Great Review: There was Mary drest in her Sunday best/And our boy Billee too'), the pseudo-folk of Stephen Foster, dainty sentiment, and pathos:

> Set my hands upon the plough,
>   My feet upon the sod;
> Turn my face towards the east
>   And thanks be to God.
>   'The Blind Ploughman'

Love, sorrow, friendship, nature, patriotism, they were all counters to be flicked into a bowl in a game of high-minded tiddly-winks. The *avant garde* was at the door with tuneless incomprehensible music, but, as Fred Weatherly, with 1,500 songs under his belt, argued:

> Why should a musician despise a simple melody and think himself great for constructing discords and dull phrases? It makes some of us say 'he does not write a melody, because he can't. He would like to write a song that the people would love and buy and make the royalties roll in. But he cannot do it, and so he poses as superior and considers the songs which the millions love inartistic'.

And there spoke the voice of the age.

CHAPTER FOUR

THE MUSIC PIRATES

THE BALLAD COMPOSERS relied on the sale of their sheet music for their incomes, and there was great consternation about the turn of the century when pirated music appeared on a massive scale. Street hawkers sold ballads originally published at up to four shillings a copy for twopence, and a vast number of popular songs were put on the market at a fraction of their proper price.

The publishers suffered as well, for their profits were made precisely from those songs that were easiest to produce. As one of the Chappell family said, all that a pirate had to do was to find an old barn and set up a printing press, and with the constant advances in print technology, presses twenty or thirty years old could be bought for a song. The wooden presses once used for the production of broadsides were still in working order, and were once more put into service.

In one sense, it served the publishers right, for sheet music was grotesquely overpriced and even on a pound to pound basis was more expensive than today. Nor were the publishers of ballads and popular music hall songs averse to sharp practice, and many pieces were deliberately priced at double their acceptable value so that they could immediately be offered at half-price. There was also a good deal of over-production, and in 1898 William Lea of Liverpool inserted the following advertisement in the *Musical Times*:

GREAT SALE OF SHEET MUSIC. Each copy clean and saleable.

150,000 copies of Songs, Pieces and Dances, by all the Great Composers.

250 Songs, Pieces and Dances	£1	5	0
500 Songs, Pieces and Dances	£2	5	0
1,000 Songs, Pieces and Dances	£4	0	0
5,000 Songs, Pieces and Dances	£19	0	0
10,000 Songs, Pieces and Dances	£36	0	0

Send at once for a Sample Parcel of £1 worth for 1s., post free. N.B.-This Music is by various Publishers, the Best Editions, and chiefly 3s. and 4s. Copies.

There was a distinction between copyright in a book and that in a piece of music, and in the case of infringement of music copyright the only action possible on the part of the owner of the copyright was seizure of illegal copies whenever they were found, a difficult operation as the pirates covered their tracks remarkably well. There had been the same problem in Victorian times when there was a great trade in pornography; the printers were rarely discovered, even though public opinion was on the side of exposure.

Chappell and Co took a leading role in trying to prise the pirates from their burrows, and they and other music publishers formed a 'Musical Copyright Association', employing strong-arm men, often retired policemen, to raid the premises of printers and also to tackle the hawkers in the streets. This led to uncomfortable moments, for the public often intervened when they saw a harmless street trader being set upon by roughs, often armed.

A Bill to amend the law of copyright was introduced by Lord Monkswell, and this passed through its various stages and became law in late 1902. It proved to be difficult to administer, and the trade in pirated music flourished unhindered. An exasperated music publisher recounted his experiences:

At 7 o'clock in the evening one of our agents had 38 copies seized at a street stall. The man in the stall swore, and said he would have more in half-an-hour. The agent went to the stall at 8.30 and seized 30 copies: at 9.45 25 copies, at 10.15 16 copies. This same publisher has had his stock seized at least a dozen times.

In some weeks publishers' agents seized 100,000 copies of pirated songs, and on one occasion 300,000 copies were taken *en masse* from a pirate publisher.

In 1903 the American composer — conductor Sousa was in London and was horror-struck by pirated editions of his works 'being sold broadcast in the streets of the city'. Michael Maybrick, who was not only the ballad composer Stephen Adams but the mayor of Ryde, was even more indignant. He wrote to the *Music Trades Review* to say that he had before him no less than seven different pirated editions of his ballad, 'The Holy City'. Loss of royalties was not compensated for by the comforting knowledge that this piece was so popular.

Pirated music became a serious threat to the very existence of music publishers, and an extreme step was taken in 1905 when twenty-one music publishers appended their names to a statement declaring that they would spend no more money on new publications or on newspaper advertisements for their stock list. Many respectable printers were thereupon thrown out of work, but the dramatic move by the publishers which threatened advertising revenue as well as hundreds of jobs in the music trade brought the attention of MPs to the state of affairs. A promising Bill had been talked out in 1903, but with mounting pressures on Parliament to do something meetings were held at which leading composers such as Parry and Elgar spoke in favour of a Bill with teeth.

Before such a Bill was passed, a long prosecution for conspiracy of a bankrupt fishmonger known as 'the Pirate King' was brought to a successful fruition, mainly through the efforts of Chappell and Co, for whom no expense was too great if it meant getting rid of the pirates. They were said to have spent £10,000 on this and other prosecutions, and in backing a Bill by T. P. O'Connor, MP for a division of Liverpool, one-time editor of *The Star* and *The Sun* and, named after himself, *T.P.'s Weekly*, which might be described as the most boring periodical ever published for gain. Notwithstanding his journalistic deficiencies, O'Connor succeeded in getting the Bill passed, and it became law in August 1906, providing sufficient penalties. The trade in pirated music was abruptly cut short, and those who still thought that the old days were here found themselves in prison with twelve months' hard labour.

In 1909 the *Sheffield Daily Telegraph* reported on a new phenomenon:

> The High Street gutter pirate has hit on a new scheme for beguiling twopences from the unwary purchaser of cheap music. 'Pantomime words and music, 2d.' is the luring legend, followed in large type with titles of popular ditties, etc., chief among them 'The Merry Widow Valse', 'Oh! Oh! Antonio', 'Love me and the, etc.,' 'Lou, Lou, Lou', and a dozen others of similar calibre. Alas! the merry widow smiles but to deceive, for on turning to the promised valse it proves to be 'The Gay Widow', companion to (in very small type) her more notorious sister (in large capitals). 'Lou, Lou, Lou', is nothing more than our old friend 'The Swanee River', and the rest of this pantomime (!) music is made up of illegible reprints from 'Scipio', Mendelssohn's 'Lied ohne Worte No. 9', Schumann's 'Wiegenlied', and 'The Harmonious Blacksmith'. The words of certain songs are printed on the cover. There is twopennyworth of fun in being victimised by the amusing fraud.

At about the same time the writer on music Percy Scholes found hawkers in the streets of Leeds selling booklets of the words and music of popular songs, only to find that the sixteen pages that comprised this booklet were identical. An interesting sidelight on a world that was always looking for something for nothing.

CHAPTER FIVE

HIGHBROWS AND LOWBROWS

THE VIEW OF the song-writer Weatherly that modern musicians despised a simple melody, and thought themselves great for constructing 'discords and dull phrases' was widespread. The Edwardian period was the age in which a gulf between composers and the public widened so much that communication was lost. This had rarely happened before. The putative neglect of Beethoven, so often treated as a classic case of misunderstanding and abandonment, never happened: one has only to look at the programmes of the Philharmonic Society to see that. During his lifetime, and afterwards, Beethoven was always strongly represented in orchestral concerts. Mendelssohn is credited with the rediscovery of Bach; Bach's B minor Mass was not given an adequate British performance until the 1870s. But Bach was never neglected; he had a minority audience which was always faithful to him, and there was a statistically predictable response to his work.

Another example of an ostensibly unjustly neglected composer was Berlioz, apparently years ahead of his time with music that soared uncomprehendingly above the heads of a Victorian audience, and it is too easily forgotten that he was championed in England by the showman pioneer of Promenade Concerts, Louis Jullien, who put on one of Berlioz's most characteristic works, *Harold in Italy*. The only people who waxed indignant against it were the music critics; the sixpenny audience liked it.

Witty as these same critics were at the expense of Wagner, the pit and gallery could not have too much of him, and in 1880 Covent Garden did the whole of the *Ring* cycle of music dramas, much to the distress of the box holders for whom Italian opera was the only genre worth attending.

These facts are worth bearing in mind; the most up-to-date music was accepted, and when one of the stalwarts of contemporary music, Franz Liszt, visited London he received a tremendous reception, even *Punch* finding him worth a few columns, a sure token of esteem. What was labelled 'The New Music' did not have to fight too hard for acceptance. Admittedly there were indications that things would change; Liszt was writing piano music in a bare, angular style that the lovers of his more romantic works would have found alien had they known about it. In Paris, Charles Alkan, born in 1813, was composing piano music containing 'technical specialities nowhere else to be found, difficulties of a titanic sort, effects peculiar to the instrument carried to the very verge of impossibility' (Edward Dannreuther writing in Grove's *Dictionary of Music and Musicians* in 1878). At the opposite extreme, the young Erik Satie (born 1866) was writing music of so pellucid a texture that the ultra-modern content of the music was concealed in simplicity.

By the opening of the twentieth century there were indications that a revolution was to take place in music. In 1894 Debussy had written *The Afternoon of a Faun* with ambiguities of tonality that would have perplexed and angered but for the quiet tone and lush orchestration. In 1896 Richard Strauss had composed *Thus Spake Zarathustra*; in 1889 his *Death and Transfiguration* had shocked the musical establishment.

The revolution predictably took place. At the Promenade Concerts in London in September 1912 Sir Henry Wood conducted the first performance of the *Five Orchestral Pieces* by Schoenberg, music in no key, apparently without a beginning, a middle, or an end, and providing nowhere for a listener to hang his hat. The critic of *The Times* was civilised and restrained; the listener 'was like a dweller in Flatland straining his mind to understand the ways of that mysterious occupant of three dimensions, Man'. No Victorian critic would have dared to have

"A MODERN OPERA."

Although this is a German cartoon, it illustrates how most people viewed modern opera. (Strand)

written in this manner, though the correspondent of *Le Temps* was more outspoken when Stravinsky's *The Rite of Spring* was performed in Paris in 1913: 'The cult of the false note has never been practised with such zeal and persistence as in this score.'

However, this book is not about Edwardian unpopular music, interesting as such a book might be, but it is important to show the ferment into which the age was thrown by the forces of the *avant garde*. Naturally this was not a movement confined to music; in 1910 the Grafton Gallery had a gap between exhibitions and put on a show of Post-Impressionist painters. Cézanne, Matisse, and Gauguin were, according to the newspapers and periodicals of the time, jejune, barbarous, imbecilic, weird, uncouth and tortuous.

The public responded to the new forces in the arts biologically; like an amoeba, it split. The good old days when a man could go

THE TRIUMPH OF GENIUS.

The terms highbrow and lowbrow were first used in the United States in 1908. *One of the characteristics of the highbrow was soulful yearning, well exemplified in this engraving.* (Cassell's Magazine)

to a first house variety show, then to a Promenade Concert or an opera, then back home for a musical evening, enjoying all and not conscious of any personality schisms, were gone for good. The terms highbrow (first used in the United States in 1908) and lowbrow were brought in; there had been no need for these words before.

These two groups began sniping at each other, and, except during World War II, when miraculously the cultural conditions of pre-Edwardian Britain were restored, they have been sniping at each other ever since. With this conflict arose the paradox of popular unpopular music (just as James Laver categorised bad good art, and good bad art), for certain kinds of work were taken up by the pretentious as a token of their intellectual superiority, and music that might have died of malnutrition flourished. At the same time there was a fad for early music, fostered by the unique Dolmetsch family, while those who eagerly took up cudgels for the school of Schoenberg, and more especially insignificant composers trying to get on the modernist bandwaggon, opted also for revivalism and, indeed, anything that was not popular.

It was easy enough to pour scorn on popular music of the period, on music-hall songs, on drawing-room ballads, and at the *chinoiserie* and Viennese *schmalz* of the musical comedy. It was easier still to mock the pretentiousness of the second-rate musical revolutionaries, and a wave of bad feeling rose up that obfuscated the situation. Genuinely adventurous spirits who honestly found that they needed a new musical language to express themselves were lumped by the cynical with the hangers-on. Worse still, they were patronised by half-baked ignoramuses anxious to be in the swim.

In many cases, musicians of modest gifts were brain-washed into believing that they ought to go modern—one could make parallels today—and introduced into their otherwise unremarkable pieces the clichés of modern music. These included the ballad composer Maude Valérie White. Occasionally a minor composer, such as Cyril Scott, best-known for his piano pieces, could apply modern touches like icing on to a nourishing fruit-cake of no great individuality, and get away with it. His salon pieces are no less reprehensible through having the odd quaint chord here and there.

In a parody of music publishers' lists, *Punch* announced a set of International Miniatures by 'Vladimir Howley': ' "The Cannibal's Carnival," *Allegro sanguinolento* is a pleasant piece of frank realism in which a strepitous figure in the bass charmingly simulates the gnashing of teeth. No. 2., "Valse Voodoo", has a cadaverous charm which is all its own', while 'Universal Orgy' 'represents the scenes enacted in the monster shops of High Street, Kensington, on the occasion of a cheap sale.' Also from the house of Slammer and Vamp was '*Pandemonium*; a Cancantana for bass solo, chorus, two gongs, four piccolos, eight trombones, and sixteen xylophones'. No doubt this was amusing in 1906, but in the days to come not altogether dissimilar combinations made their only-too-real appearance on the concert platform.

As is evident from *Punch*, music-lovers were repelled as much by the barbaric force and violent rhythms of the new music as by the intellectual content. In the space of a few pre-World War I years the public were subjected to, not the fiction of 'Vladimir Howley', but the deliberate harshness and brutality of Bela Bartók's *Allegro barbaro* (1911), Stravinsky's *Petrushka* (1911) and sections of Richard Strauss's *Salome* (1905) and *Elektra* (1909) in which the unsympathetic could see an unhealthy preoccupation with perversion and cruelty.

The new music arrived surreptitiously. The year's music for 1903 shows little evidence of disturbing elements. The main events were three cycles of Wagner's *Ring* at Covent Garden, the first London performance of Elgar's *Dream of Gerontius* at Westminster Cathedral, the Richard Strauss festival at St James's Hall, and the debut of a talented lady violinist, Marie Hall. The various festivals were doing unalarming oratorios, the fate of which was to be one performance each, ever—who has heard of Vosbach's *Page and King's Daughter* performed at the Middlesbrough Festival?—and the customary Handel festival had its predictable success at the Crystal Palace. Novelties at the Three Choirs Festival, held at Hereford in 1903, were Coleridge-Taylor's *Atonement*, Cowen's *Indian Rhapsody*, and Bantock's *Christus*. The old firm were busy at the Albert Hall for the Royal Choral Society's season—Sullivan, Parry, and Cowen. At the opera houses there was nothing more startling than *Tristan und Isolde*. Everything had its place, and music that was not well-worn was soporific.

In many ways, the 'serious' music of the first years of Edward's reign was as undemanding as the fashionable shop ballad, and music that asked some effort of the listener did not get it. This

Opposite: Richard Strauss's Elektra *was produced in 1910, both a promise and a warning. The advertisement for Edison phonographs at the foot of the programme is somewhat impertinent; it would be a very long time before the recording apparatus could cope with the demands of modern music. (Courtesy Victoria and Albert Museum)*

threw the diarist W. N. P. Barbellion into a frenzy:

Beethoven's Fifth Symphony

This symphony always works me up into an ecstasy; in ecstatic sympathy with its dreadfulness I could stand up in the balcony and fling myself down passionately into the arena below. Yet there were women sitting alongside me today—knitting! It so annoyed and irritated me that at the end of the first movement I got up and sat elsewhere. They would have sat knitting at the foot of the Cross, I suppose. At the end of the second movement, two or three other women got up and went home to tea! It would have surprised me no more to have seen a cork extract itself from its bottle and promenade.

OUR ORCHESTRAL SOCIETY.—*The Rector.* "Oh, *piano*, Mr. Brown! *Pi-an-o* "   *M*
Brown. " *Piano* be blowed! I've come here to enjoy myself!"

It is refreshing to realise that there were music-lovers who participated in home music and to whom the term 'chamber music' carried pleasurable overtones. (Punch)

He. "Awfully jolly concert, wasn't it? Awfully jolly thing by that fellow - what's his name ?—something like Doorknob." *She.* "*Doorknob!* Whom *do* you mean? I only know of Beethoven, Mozart, Wagner, Handel——" *He.* "That's it! Handel. I knew it was something you caught hold of!"

Many people tried to keep up with classical music for the sake of their loved ones or those they were trying to impress. A cartoon with more than a flavour of truth. (Punch)

For such concertgoers as Barbellion, a loner without any wish to associate with a clique, there was excitement and promise in the vitality of the new music that was gradually getting a hearing, and an instinctive desire to compare it, not with the acknowledged masterpieces, but with the humdrum contemporaries, the lacklustre examples of provincial oratorio, the remorseless round of Italian operas, and the ramshackle musical comedies. Highbrow was a title that one wore with pride, to differentiate oneself from the somnolent. It was only a step to associating oneself not only with the meaningful advance guard speaking a new language and letting it be known that it mattered not whether their works had an audience, but with the hangers-on.

The eagerness to be included with the elect was not confined to listeners, and writers on music were as easily taken in by the modish and the high-falutin'. In a 1909 programme note to a recently performed overture by one of the new wave of English composers, the analysis ended with the words: 'The last note is the low E of the basses, bass clarinet, harp and tamtam. This note is based on material supplied by the composer.' In another analytical programme of the period, the provider of notes to Liszt's transcription of the waltz from Gounod's *Faust* spread himself out to forty-three lines. Unfortunately he chose to describe Liszt's 'Mephisto Waltz' which was not on the programme.

The self-conscious highbrows were drawn mainly from the middle orders of society. Because of the fluctuating terms of reference they could conceal deep ignorance of modern works that they were rapturously applauding, but when espousing the cause of music of the past they were more vulnerable, as a comment in the *Musical Times* of September 1912 shows:

> Not long ago at a Symphony Concert I heard a lady solemnly assure a friend by her side at the close of the first movement of a Beethoven Symphony that that was the end of the Symphony; and when the second movement began she was equally emphatic that that was the next item on the programme—which happened to be one of Elgar's 'Bavarian Dances'! She was very concerned because the promised interval was being omitted.

The lower echelons had their tastes determined by tunes played on barrel-pianos in the streets, by street bands, at the music hall, and by disc musical boxes in the public houses—but this was in London. In the provinces there was a great emphasis on the poor participating in music. The brass bands of the north of England drew their men from industry, and working men's choirs were phenomena little known south of the Trent. Naturally, the London poor were acquainted with the tunes from musical comedy, for as soon as they were hits they were transferred to whatever mechanical reproducing machines were available—excluding the gramophone. Not for a long time to come would the gramophone be a familiar object in the working-class home.

For the upper classes, music *qua* music was not something that was wildly fashionable. There was a certain cachet in frequenting opera, and musical evenings, recitals by celebrities such as Mark Hambourg, Backhaus, Lamond and de Pachmann, and commands to the great houses to hear Melba or Patti were borne with fortitude rather than enthusiasm. The upper classes' response to music had, like that of their king, something of a low profile about it. Commitment had overtones of bad form, and although, of course, there was the occasional lapse, the invasion of the moderns was treated by the raising of an eyebrow.

One of the few means through which the poor could hear good music was the disc musical box, a popular feature of public houses. (Courtesy Graham Webb)

How We "Do" the Opera

AND YET THEY SAY WE ARE NOT A MUSICAL NATION!

DRAWN AT COVENT GARDEN BY NORMAN MORROW

A fad could involve society in being forced to hear modern music. The Diaghilev ballet of 1911 was something that one *had* to see, and patrons were subjected to fiery music, dash and colour. But this uncomfortable sleep-killing music was rarely sought out. That was left to intellectuals, Bohemians, suburbanites, or whatever epithet was topical at the time.

The age saw an upsurge in middle-class culture. The middle classes, for the first time, stopped emulating their betters, and in the newly formed garden cities and in the outer London suburbs they evolved their own life style, involving ping-pong, ju-jitsu, golf, operatic and dramatic societies, folk song, and a wide interest in the arts. Art nouveau found a secure hold, and the intellectual life was pursued hampered only by the need of the bread-winner to work a nine till five day in the City. No doubt there must have been moments of indecision when a husband came back on one of the new electric tramcars to hear the ghostly croaking of a gramophone star such as Caruso or three cricket balls whizzed about a zinc bath (a recommended way of emulating thunder for amateur theatricals).

It had been the middle classes in the cheaper seats in the London opera houses who had applauded Wagner and made him acceptable. Similarly they were the first to encounter Russian ballet (at the Coliseum in 1909) and Schoenberg at the Proms.

Were the Edwardian middle classes just musical snobs? Certainly the aspirations of the lower-middles, as epitomised by H. G. Wells's Mr Polly, were real enough, but with the sudden emergence of new categories of music, attempts at evaluation were largely beyond them, as they were for the critics. The lower middle classes underwent a good deal of discomfort at the Promenade Concerts to hear Henry J. Wood conducting his mixed bag of music, and the Proms themselves encouraged a peculiar breed of musical snob, the person who boasted that he or she had not missed a Prom in years and who took a masochistic pleasure in standing on the packed floor on a hot evening to

Opposite: There was a certain cachet about frequenting opera. The action on the stage was the least important part of it. (The Bystander)

The Queen's Hall, Langham Place, the home of the Promenade Concerts of Henry J. Wood. It was destroyed in World War II. (Pictorial London)

listen to a programme which commonly lasted twice as long as an ordinary symphony concert. The contempt of the promenader for the music-lovers who sat in the gallery and circle of the Queen's Hall was as perfidious as the haughtiness of the addicts of Italian opera towards their Wagner-loving brethren.

The foreigner visiting Edwardian England would have found more evidence of the enjoyment and appreciation of good music in out-of-the-way places than in the stuffy West End concert halls and opera houses. The West End halls, wrote Thomas Burke in his *Nights in Town*, 'are unhappily situated. The dismal Bond Street holds one, another stands cheek by jowl with Marlborough Police Court, and the other two are stuck deep in the melancholic greyness of Wigmore Street. All are absurdly inaccessible.' Burke is no more kind about London opera houses:

> The Opera in London is really more of a pageant than a musical function. The front of the house frequently claims more attention than the stage . . . The men stand up in the stalls and fix opera-glasses on the bare shoulders and necks of the women. The women lean to one another and they talk cold, corrosive talk about those others. They carve up their sisters' souls for the amusement of their men . . .

Burke suggested that opera was more enjoyed at the Old Vic's grand opera season in the Waterloo Road, where one could get a box for one and sixpence and a gallery seat for twopence. The orchestra was good without being outstanding, and the singers were more than tolerable. The audience was drawn from the lower-middles and even the improved working classes, dressed in working clothes and smoking 'cut Cavendish' (though the significance of this social note is lost in the 1970s). The choir was drawn from local talent, and was lively and enthusiastic.

For classical music without great names conducting one could go to the People's Palace in Whitechapel for its Saturday evening concerts, or the Surrey Masonic Hall in Camberwell, or an obscure concert hall in Vincent Square, or even park and pavilion concerts operated by the London County Council. Good music was not just Caruso in Covent Garden and a handful of prestige conductors and orchestras pinned in a circumscribed part of fashionable London.

A different aspect of intellectual life concerned the revival of old music. Many thought that this was antiquarianism for the sake of it, a self-indulgent foray into the past, using old, inefficient instruments long since replaced.

For classical music without great names conducting one could go to the People's Palace, Whitechapel, for their Saturday evening concerts.
(Around London)

Another outlet for good music was the park concerts operated by the London County Council. (Around London)

It would be unjust to pour scorn on a commendable movement to re-evaluate music of Tudor and Stuart times, and there were men involved who were doing immensely valuable and scholarly work. Between 1889 and 1902 G. E. P. Arkwright (1864–1944) issued twenty-five volumes of old English music, comprising reprints of sets of madrigals, songs by Blow and Purcell, and other completely forgotten works. Arkwright was also editor of the short-lived *The Musical Antiquary* (1909–13); it is reasonable to assign the failure of this magazine to Arkwright's misinterpretation of the feverish interest in old music, in his inability to see that those most vocal in their adoration of such music were those who moved away to some other musical arena when the craze died.

Another pioneer in republishing old music was W. Barclay Squire of the British Museum, who edited a considerable series of British and European madrigals between 1895 and 1913. The Reverend Dr E. H. Fellowes's massive thirty-six-volume edition of English madrigals falls somewhat outside our period—this edition was published between 1913 and 1924. An interest in madrigals was proof that one was at the very summit of high-browdom, but most of the climbers preferred to remain on the lower slopes, with the more easily appreciated instrumental music. In 1890 that best of all music critics, Bernard Shaw, wrote after a concert:

During the performance of an old overture composed by

one of the minor Bachs I was annoyed by what I took to be the jingling of a bell-wire somewhere; but it turned out to be Dr. Parry playing the cembalo part on a decrepit harpsichord.

The key man in the revival of interest in instrumental music of Tudor and Stuart times was Eugene Arnold Dolmetsch (1858–1940), aided and abetted by the musicologist J. A. Fuller-Maitland, who was disgusted with the way music was going. The new music was a 'welter' and 'the mess that the young people seemed to be making of what had been the fairest of the arts'.

Dolmetsch was a Messiah to whom the highbrows fled; these came from the upper-middle levels of society with a strong flavouring of university and the professions. This old music, they thought, was the true popular music, and if the masses could be weaned from their music-hall song or the tradesmen from their devotion to musical comedy then surely this fresh, piquant music would make headway? Parry thought this of folk music as well but, unfortunately, he was wrong. Quality, as any balladmonger could tell him, was a negligible element in the economics and propagation of popular music.

Dolmetsch and Fuller-Maitland had a hatred of modern music. Regarding Fuller-Maitland, this was a pity, for he was one of the most knowledgeable writers on music of the period, and his service to Elizabethan keyboard music can hardly be over-praised. His re-publication of the *Fitzwilliam Virginal Book* in 1899 was a key event in musical scholarship.

Dolmetsch also loathed professionalism, and at a concert he gave in Cambridge he showed his lutes and viols, and said:

> The old people used to make music for themselves, in a room just like this. Now we pay to hear *noise*; we do not hear music, it is noise we hear! What I am going to play to you is awfully beautiful, awfully simple, but really quite beyond the reach of the modern people.

The narrator is the novelist and essayist A. C. Benson: 'Then some odd tinkling things were played on virginals and lute—sounds as

if one had shaken up a cage of mice and canaries together.'
Benson felt a curious mixture of admiration and despair, with a
strong desire to giggle. It was 'real and yet fanatical', and he
went away with the absurdity of it uppermost in his mind. 'The
collection of people listening with grotesque earnestness to these
very odd sounds, the deliberate antiquity of it all, the sweeping
aside all the progress of the art, and the sense that they probably
found the same emotion in it as we find in the new music.'

Another person who found the Dolmetsch concerts odd was
Katherine Bradley, who with Edith Cooper formed the composite
'Michael Field', devoting their lives to Poetry with a capital P:

> In the Dolmetsch concert-room I have passed some of the
> most acutely miserable moments of my life . . . If the instru-
> ments sang I should be content: they buzz. There was one
> little French song that rose up, a thin little plaint to the
> heavens—then the infinite self-absorption of the bees began
> again . . . The audience is the quaintest I have ever met—
> misshapen, defeated, ugly people, manqué every soul among
> them, asking of life to be insignificant.

Early music was seen by many as the one simple answer to the
turbulent and asymmetrical arts ushered in by the twentieth
century. As with the folk music revival, it was thought to be a
form that would be appreciated by all. But its advocates were in
thrall to the mistaken doctrine of the Victorian optimists—give
the people the best and they will know it for what it is, and
accept it. The acidity of the comments of Benson and Miss
Bradley only demonstrated to the enthusiasts the humbug of the
artistic, or at worst aesthetic, middle classes. Eventually, it was
hoped, the message of the old music would win through, though
revivals of folk music and Tudor and Stuart music never had a
chance. They were smothered by the most strenuous enemies of
popular music, and only in recent years have elements of them
emerged as invaluable parts of the pop music spectrum, modified
to suit the age, and with the hard corners knocked off in precisely
the way the Victorians and the Edwardians dealt with their
musical heritage.

CHAPTER SIX

THE MUSICAL EVENING

THE MUSICAL EVENING was more of a Victorian than an Edwardian institution, more of a social than a musical event, but it persisted often against all the odds because it enabled the middle classes to exercise their prerogative of emulating the upper classes. The middle classes could not get Patti or Melba to sing to them, or afford the infant-prodigy pianists to play to them in their own homes, so they had to do the best they could with the talents of friends and acquaintances.

A musical evening lacked the daunting formality of a dinner party, but there was an etiquette to keep. The guests left their music in the hall or, if they were female, took their music cases up to the bedroom. It was bad form to be too eager to play, but it was considered an insult if the hostess refused to allow guests to perform their party pieces.

Performers had to gauge the taste of the host and hostess to a hair's-breadth. There were houses where music-hall songs went down well, others where imitations of Albert Chevalier or Harry Champion were greeted with at best half-hearted applause and at worst a chilly silence. 'Any Old Iron' could be construed as the epitome of good fellowship or distinctly common.

The staple diet of the musical evening was the ballad, and because so many ballads were published amateurs eagerly read reports in the newspapers to find out what was good and what was not. Many of them frequented ballad concerts, the most

The Infant Prodigy has reached the middle of an exceedingly difficult pianoforte solo, and one of those dramatic pauses of whi
the celebrated composer is so fond has occurred.
Kindly, but undiscerning, Old Lady. "PLAY SOMETHING YOU KNOW, DEARIE."

There were not enough genuine infant prodigies to go round, so musical
evenings had to do the best they could with what talent there was available
(and consequent misunderstanding). (Punch)

important of which were held at the Queen's Hall, and the
advertisements in, for example, the *Daily Telegraph* would list
singers who were performing the most popular ballads on the
same evening all over the country.

In rating whether a ballad was suitable for performance at a
musical evening the amateur would rely on the singer rather than
the composer. A ballad sung by Clara Butt was guaranteed a good
sale. The Edwardian middle classes were not so keen as the
Victorians on ballads dealing with unrequited love, and were
more inclined to those dealing with mysterious out-of-the-way
places and, in contrast, home. When 'Little Grey Home in the
West' was first sung at a ballad concert, the singer did not think

highly of it, but it was fervently encored and became a success overnight. Those singers who liked dialect songs, but were uncertain whether pseudo-Cockney would go down well, had a hoard of rustic songs to choose from, and there was always a favourable reception for rollicking sea songs such as Weatherly's 'The Glory of the Sea' (O come you, sailor, from the South? Or from the black North Sea?).

Although singers were most plentiful at musical evenings, there was usually a pianist or two, and it was customary for the performer to run his or her hands up and down the keyboard in a cascade of notes. Known as the 'butterfly touch', this was a signal for conversation to cease, or at least drop in volume. It

Although singers were most plentiful, there was usually a pianist or two at musical evenings. (The King)

was generally agreed at musical evenings that expression or 'touch' were more important than complete accuracy, and pieces that sounded more difficult than they were were always assured of a welcome. There were plenty of fantasias on popular operatic airs to choose from, in which the tune was surrounded by a comfortable welter of easy-to-play arpeggios that lay nicely beneath the hands.

Basically there are four kinds of piano music: the elementary teaching piece, the sentimental equivalent of the royalty ballad, the salon piece, and the difficult serious work. The drawing-room pianist's repertoire could be taken from all four groups. There were certain plums concealed in pieces of considerable difficulty, an example being the first movement of the 'Moonlight' sonata. Many pianists, having got through this and feeling that the occasion was propitious would tackle the second movement, which falls reasonably well beneath the hands, though the trio has syncopated rhythms that can creep up on an amateur, and then the finale, which can be bluffed through by an average pianist. Similarly the 'Pathétique' sonata, with the impressive and tolerably easy chordal opening, was worth an attempt. Chopin's G minor Ballade, to begin with, is not difficult, and the attractive tune in the middle section can scarcely be resisted by a doleful pianist, but half-way through, before the repeat of the 'big' tune, there is passagework that demands the utmost technical command, and no doubt there are many who have heard, wincing in their seats, a mediocre pianist trying to scramble through the extremely taxing chromatic double octaves on the last page.

Salon pieces could be either soft or loud, sentimental or pompous. The Edwardians inherited a vast stock of salon music, and, although the composers are unknown and rarely figure in musical reference books, until quite recently certain pieces of music have remained in publisher's catalogues, music that called for the minimum of effort and maximum of effect, no awkward bridge passages in fourths, plenty of octaves but not much jumping about, and a singing diatonic tune somewhere. Two showy pieces that were still on sale after World War II were 'The Battle of Prague' by Kotzwara, a 'bondage' masochist who was left hanging up by a London prositute when she went out shopping and who was dead when she got back, and 'The Maiden's Prayer' by Thekla Badarzewska, an early nineteenth-century Polish composer who died young.

Of a slightly higher standard was 'La Pluie de Perles' by George Alexander Osborne (1806–93). Twelve different publishers were licensed to produce editions of it. At a fashionable party the composer was asked to play something, and he responded with 'La Pluie de Perles', only to have his rendition greeted by laughter. He was less indignant when he discovered that prior to his arrival four other pianists had played the same piece.

Another composer for drawing-room pianists was Brinley Richards (1819–85), responsible for 'Warblings at Dawn' and 'Warblings at Eve', while 'Les Cloches du Monastère'—French titles gave class—by Lefébure-Wély was also extremely popular. Joseph Ascher, composer of the ballad 'Alice, Where Art Thou?', had a long list of salon titles to his credit, including 'Clochettes', and 'Cascade de Roses', and he, rare amongst the breed, realised that they were, as he put it himself, 'atrocious, and so difficult to write'. His great ambition was to put before the public the works he had written without his tongue in his cheek and which the publishers would not touch.

An interesting guide to the kind of modern piano music played at musical evenings is furnished by the review columns of the musical press. Of R. H. Bellairs's 'Barcarole' for piano, the *Musical News* critic wrote: 'A melodious solo of medium difficulty, decidedly useful. It is neatly figured and phrased, falls under the hands well, and especially affords good practice for the left.' 'Six Tone Pictures' by Claude Parnell were dismissed as 'aimless and disjointed', and the 'March of Empire' and 'March of Destiny', written to supplement the store of works for the patriotic market built up by the Boer War, would 'pass muster if played by a military band'.

Even in the world of salon piano music, modernism was rearing its ugly head, and Roloff's 'Russian Lullaby' was attacked for 'the awful reiterated major seventh'. Cyril Scott's 'Barcarolle' had 'occasional lapses into discord [that] give one the shudders', while Reginald Somerville's 'Automobile Valse' was an ill-timed

excursion into the fashionable. There was easy-to-play modern music that was acceptable both at recitals and at musical evenings, such as Debussy's 'Arabesques', but anything more advanced than these graceful pieces was unequivocally eschewed.

The piano still occupied its place in the drawing-room. Nearly 20,000 pianos were being imported annually, for it was an article of faith that German pianos were the best (surprisingly, nearly 5,000 organs and harmoniums were also being brought in every year). Pianos were not expensive, and high-quality second-hand grand pianos were available at realistic prices (in 1911 the *Music Trades Record* advertised grands by Broadwood, Hagspiel, and Bord at between £14 and £16).

The greatest threat to the amateur pianist was the Pianola and the player-piano, which reached their zeniths during the period. Using perforated paper rolls and the power of air, reproducing pianos represented the ultimate triumph of mechanical music. In 1897 the Pianola piano-player was perfected in America; this was not a piano-like instrument complete in itself, but was rolled up to the keyboard of a piano, and the first instruments of this type were exceedingly cumbersome and often as large as the piano itself. Within ten years the original Pianola had run its course, rendered obsolete by new developments.

In 1901 a method had been discovered of packing all the trappings of a reproducing piano into the piano itself, and within a year the Aeolian Company of New York was advertising 'The Pianola Piano—The First Complete Piano'. In 1904 a grand piano with a player action was produced. In America 2½ million player-pianos were sold between 1904 and 1930, and although the British did not subscribe to this instrument with such enthusiasm the player-piano became very popular. Shortly before World War I the reproducing piano was invented by the firms of Duo-Art and Ampico; using these instruments, not only was the music played, but a performance by a specific pianist with all the tone gradations was faithfully rendered.

Opposite: Five thousand organs and harmoniums were imported every year. This grotesque instrument cost a mere £22. (London Home)

The Pianola piano-player was perfected in 1897, and proved very popular. The early models were rolled on to a piano keyboard, but later ones incorporated the mechanism inside the piano case. (The King)

There were other mechanical musical instruments available to those with sufficient interest and money. In Britain the barrel-piano was more often employed outdoors than in the home; the barrel-piano worked on the same principle as a musical box—a revolving barrel with pins striking against keyed teeth or wires—and the gay, jangly sound was more suited to the public house than to the drawing-room. Organ-type instruments operated by paper rolls or folded card were sold, but many people found their tone tiresome, and although organettes were much cheaper than Pianolas (push-on variety—£65 in 1901) they had a restricted circulation in an age when the harmonium, the tone of which resembled that of the organette, represented all that was worst in the period that had just gone. Self-playing violins, such as the Phonoliszt-Violina of 1910 comprising a player-piano and three vertically mounted violins, were expensive, little-seen curiosities. Their more mundane brother, the Automatic Virtuoso, consisting of one self-playing violin operated electro-magnetically by a music roll, was put on display in Waring and Gillow's store in 1908 and created a sensation. But gogglers were more numerous than buyers—it cost the equivalent of between £700 and £800. As there are about twenty self-playing violins in Britain at present, it is clear that a few succumbed to the temptation of having one of these instruments.

There were also mechanical zithers and harps, and the former can be seen in antique shops quite frequently, proving that there was some demand for them, if only as toys for the children. The roll-playing mechanical accordion and concertina also received an amount of publicity in inverse proportion to sales.

During the Victorian period the ability to play a musical instrument other than a piano was an asset to the well-bred gentleman, and amateur male flautists were by no means uncommon. The supply of amateur male instrumentalists dried up towards the close of the nineteenth century, and only one instrument other than the piano was regarded with favour by young middle-class men—the banjo, which enjoyed a revival owing to the introduction of ragtime. (The banjo was first employed in 1846 when the nigger minstrels came over to Britain from the United States.) The banjo was sporty and not difficult to play, and

The concertina was a working man's instrument, ideal for proletarian musical junkets. (Cassell's Magazine)

the chords of the new dance music were simple and easy to pick up. However, the tone of the musical evening usually precluded the use of a banjo, and those who would have liked to have played it were forced to act as 'turners-over' of piano music, a role much coveted when the pianist was a nubile young lady.

The standard of music at a musical evening was, of course, variable, as was the quality of the performances. More often than not it was entertainment on a shoestring, though there were groups of instrumentalists ready, and eager, to give class to a soirée, such as the Armour Quintette of West Ealing, London, which advertised in the *Musical News* that they were 'open to engagements for concerts, at homes'.

Ballad concerts often included German *lieder* and 'art' songs, but musical evenings were usually top-heavy with the maudlin and the lachrymose. It was easier for an indifferent singer to play on the listeners' feelings than give them an aesthetic experience:

> Take my head on your shoulder, Daddy,
>   Turn your face to the west,
> 'Tis just the hour when the sky turns gold,
>   The hour that Mother loved best.
> The day has been long without you, Daddy,
>   You've been such a while away,
> And you are tired of your work, Daddy,
>   As I am tired of my play.

Musical evenings also offered opportunities for flirtation not open to the Miss Butts at the Queen's Hall:

> If no one ever marries me,
>   And I don't see why they should,

All the world is singing FAMILY JOURNAL SONGS

The words and music of a Charming Song FREE each week

Songs were distributed not only in sheet-music form but through the popular weekly press. Most of the songs published in newspapers were very bad indeed.
(Woman's World)

For nurse says I'm not pretty,
  And I'm seldom very good;
If no one ever marries me,
  I shan't mind very much,
I shall buy a squirrel in a cage,
  And a little rabbit-hutch . . .

There were also musical monologues, the narrator accompanying himself at the piano, and Kipling's 'Gunga Din' came in for some harsh treatment. Treasuries of suitable works for recitation continued to come from the presses, almost every one of them featuring 'The Siege of Lucknow', and seasoned hands at musical evenings winced when a gentleman—it was more often a gentleman than a lady—got out his grubby bit of paper. Recitations

A musical evening with audience participation. Don't call us, we'll call you!

were a penance that vied with musical ladies singing their own compositions or cocky young girls trying out Mendelssohn's *Songs Without Words*, perhaps the best-selling piano music of all time (one girl wrote to the music correspondent of *Girls' Own Journal* asking if she knew of anyone who would play this music to her for sixpence an hour).

There were always advertisements in the musical press by musicians offering to revise compositions by amateurs, and well-known lyric writers received many requests, and occasionally demands, to put their words to music. The interest in writing ballads is understandable when one considers the great profits that could come from it, and the contempt of the music reviewers, if it ever got published, was a worthwhile risk. 'Good-night, Beloved', words by Longfellow, that mine of goodies, music by T. Atherling, was savaged in the press ('They have little to recommend them, the music being quite ordinary and fitting the words clumsily'), but no doubt Mr Atherling tried again. The manager of the music publishers, Augener's, commented that whenever a foreigner had a hit, 200 English composers sent him imitations. And many of these imitations had been tried out at musical evenings where there was a captive audience.

Nevertheless, an institution does not persist if it is not wanted, and musical evenings with audience participation went right on into the gramophone age, not only for the buffet supper that followed the entertainment but because the Edwardians, like the Victorians, enjoyed making music for themselves, a phenomenon that many today would, unfortunately, find difficult to understand.

CHAPTER SEVEN

THE GRAMOPHONE

IN 1908, CASSELL'S MAGAZINE published an article on the gramophone in which the author stated:

> Not even the prophetic genius of Shakespeare, who fore-shadowed an electric girdle round the earth, ever imagined that there would come a time when the human voice, and music of all kinds, would be capable of exact reproduction. Step by step the Gramophone has been perfected, until today, the thrilling notes of Melba, or the exquisite violin strains of Mischa Elman, can be reproduced with absolute exactitude for the benefit of millions who may never have listened to either of those great artistes in the flesh. Every possible defect seems to have been eliminated.

Apart from the impossibility of any, even Shakespeare, foreshadowing an electric girdle round the earth, there are errors of fact in every line. Exact reproduction was impossible, absolute exactitude was a downright lie, and every possible defect remained, so that a record was a parody rather than a faithful repeat of voice or instrument. However, the gramophone was alone in its field; there was nothing to compare it with. The phonograph, which never caught on in England as it had done in America and France, was no more efficient.

The inventor of the gramophone was Emile Berliner, and in

WHAT WILL YOU DO

IN THE

LONG, COLD, DARK, SHIVERY EVENINGS,

WHEN YOUR HEALTH AND CONVENIENCE COMPEL YOU TO STAY

INDOORS?

WHY!!! HAVE A PHONOGRAPH, OF COURSE.

It is the FINEST ENTERTAINER in the WORLD.

There is nothing equal to it in the whole Realm
of Art.
It imitates any and every Musical Instrument,
any and every natural sound, faithfully:

the **HUMAN VOICE**, the **NOISE OF THE CATARACT**, the **BOOM OF THE GUN**, the **VOICES OF BIRDS OR ANIMALS.**

From

£2 2s.

THE GREATEST MIMIC.

A Valuable Teacher of Acoustics.   Most Interesting to Old or Young   A Pleasure
and Charm to the Suffering, bringing to them the Brightness and Amusements of
the outside World by its faithful reproductions of Operas, New Songs, Speeches, &c

EVERY HOME WILL sooner or later have its **PHONOGRAPH** as a **NECESSITY.**

HAVE YOURS NOW; you will enjoy it longer.

Brought within the reach of every family by Mr. Edison's last production at **£2 2s.**

Send for our Illustrated Catalogues to

EDISON - BELL CONSOLIDATED PHONOGRAPH CO., LD.,

Or to our Licensees—   39, **Charing Cross Road, W.C.**

EDISONIA LD., 25 to 22, Banner Street, and City Show-Rooms, 21, Cheapside, E.C., LONDON.

*Despite massive advertising campaigns, the phonograph never really
caught on in Britain and was never a viable alternative to the gramophone.*

(Illustrated London News)

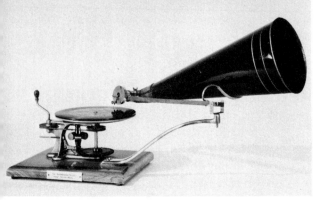

An early hand-driven gramophone. Erratic tempos added another element to what were very inefficient instruments. (Courtesy Science Museum)

order to cash in on his European rights before rival inventors could steal his market he sent William Owen to London. Owen took rooms at the Hotel Cecil to exhibit the Berliner gramophone to a stream of visitors, and in 1898 the Gramophone Company was started with a capital of £15,000. The machines were to be imported from the United States, and record pressings were to come from a factory in Hanover, Germany, that Berliner intended building.

The Gramophone Company looked around for a trade mark. The first depicted an angel writing with a quill pen on a gramophone record, but the second eventually proved much more satisfactory. Owen bought from the artist Francis Barraud the picture 'An Encore Too Many' which showed a terrier with its head cocked listening to a phonograph, on condition that Barraud painted the phonograph out and put a gramophone in. Only after this picture had hung on his walls for a while was it realised that this would make a splendid logos for the new firm.

By early 1899 the Hanover factory was ready for full-scale production, with fourteen presses. At this stage records were seven inches in diameter, single-sided, with the title and recording artist etched in the centre of the record. The paper label was introduced in 1900.

Using American promotional methods—taking a full-page advertisement in the *Daily Mail*—the Gramophone Company created an immense stir, and encouraged by preliminary success decided to go into the typewriter business as well, though this proved a failure. Recording specialists, trained in America, scoured Europe for likely talent. Chaliapin, the great Russian singer, was one of the first to be booked up, and it was decided to sell his records for £1 each on a special red label. These were snapped up like hot cakes, and prestige labels became a speciality of the Gramophone Company. In 1902 Caruso was recorded in Milan, receiving £100 for ten arias; before his death in 1921 he had earned more than £400,000 from his records.

It may have been fortuitous that operatic recordings should have occupied the attentions of the Gramophone Company; it may have been that the recording engineers, and the company's key man, Fred Gaisberg, found it a pleasurable as well as a rewarding occupation roaming Europe. Certainly the home of the gramophone, America, had shown little concern for operas. The automatic phonograph parlours of the 1890s that had sprouted like mushrooms had catered for a much lower musical taste. The star attraction of the parlours was a series of spoken records by Russell Hunting featuring an Irishman named Casey and a straight man, Hunting playing both roles. 'Casey as a judge', 'Casey takes the census' and 'Casey at the telephone' enjoyed enormous success. For those with more rarified tastes there were Sousa marches, the nigger minstrel Billy Golden doing 'Turkey in de Straw' and the negro, George Johnson, 'The Whistling Coon'

A factor that also predisposed the Gramophone Company towards quality music was the appointment in 1901 of Landon Ronald as musical adviser, a post that he held until 1938. Although this episode in his life is all but ignored in his autobiography, Landon Ronald played a great part in giving the gramophone-buying public an interest in snippets of opera (though as early as 1903 a complete opera had been recorded).

Landon Ronald was born in 1873, and his first appearance as a musician was as solo pianist in the wordless musical play *L'Enfant Prodigue* in 1890, leading to a season at Covent Garden. In 1908, after several years as a highly-rated conductor, he was appointed conductor of the New Symphony Orchestra (later the Royal Albert Hall Orchestra), and in 1910 he became principal of the Guildhall school of music. He was a son of Henry Russell (1812–1900), singer, pianist, author, and composer, popular in music hall and drawing-room with rousing patriotic ditties such as 'A Life on the Ocean Wave' and the emotional 'Woodman,

Spare That Tree'. Ronald had a best-selling ballad to his credit, 'Down in the Forest', and wrote many songs distinguished by their musicianship.

It is probable that, but for the prestigious figure of Landon Ronald, the tycoons of the Gramophone Company would have plumped for the easy option and made the list bottom-heavy with popular music. Landon Ronald also encouraged good musicians to participate in recording, and the operatic stars knew that however primitive the recording equipment, the musical adviser would ensure that the results were not too catastrophic.

Chaliapin had recorded on ten-inch discs; the celebrated singer Francesco Tamagno received a £2,000 advance when he recorded thirty-five twelve-inch records in three weeks in 1903. Nineteen titles were issued at £1 each; a full-page advertisement was taken in the *Daily Telegraph* to promote them, and the Gramophone Company addressed dealers in the following terms:

The £1 record has raised the whole tone of the gramophone

Adelina Patti did not find singing rubbish detrimental to her career. She bought a castle in Wales on the proceeds. (Ludgate)

business. It has brought into the trade new customers who will remain, if carefully nursed and judiciously attended to, a constant source of income to the dealer.

If money was a token of prestige—and it was through every aspect of Edwardian life—Melba topped Tamagno. Melba's discs were out on sale in 1904 at a guinea each with special 'Melba labels' printed on mauve paper. Adelina Patti was also recruited; living in stately splendour in a Welsh castle, she insisted that the Gramophone Company sent their men to record her there. Her records were also retailed at a guinea apiece, but to those who enthusiastically bought them they proved something of a disappointment, for Patti, who had sung for £1,000 a time, was now sixty-two.

When one considers that the average weekly wage at this time was not much more than £1 a week, the records of Melba, Caruso, and Patti were certainly not bought by the masses. However, music hall stars—Dan Leno, Eugene Stratton, and R. G. Knowles, together with the music hall ladies, Ada Reeve, Vesta Tilley, and Marie Lloyd—were being recruited to record for the lower end of the market.

Compared with the techniques involved in putting the operatic singers on record, the methods used for music-hall celebrities were casual and improvised. Dan Leno arrived without his accompanist, so the recording technician had to officiate; Dan Leno was also a champion clog-dancer, so he was hoisted on to a table to record the taps. George Mozart arrived with a heavy theatrical hamper; a red-nosed comedian of the old school, Mozart could not get the feel of it until he had climbed into costume.

The London studios were in the Coburg Hotel. The recording instrument was placed on a high stage, and from it led a long thin trumpet which acted as a microphone. A piano was positioned on a high platform which had wheels so that it could be sited where it was most needed. There was an additional platform for any orchestral accompanists.

There were artistes who were merely keeping their names before the public by making records, such as the musical-comedy star, Edna May. Away from the theatre, with its atmosphere,

PATTI

Madame Adelina Patti's Legacy to the Wor

"HER GRAMOPHONE RECORDS

In an interview which appeared in "The Graphic" of Nov. 24th, Madame Patti expressed herself regarding the Gramophone in these te

"Caruso sings to me on the Gramophone. And what an invention that is! The old records that they took of my voice were good, but those which they are just bringing out are perfect. I have heard nothing better, unless it be Caruso's *Pagliacci* record, and that of the duet from *I due Foscari*, which he sings with Scotti. In these days, you see, even in the wilds of Wales one can keep in touch with the outside world."

PATTI has also written the following letter:

"I am quite satisfied that future generations should hear my voice by means of the Gramophone, and I think the records are faithful reproductions of my voice."

Gramophone Records recently made by Madame Adelina Patti.

12-inch Records.

03053 Home, Sweet Home (*Sir H. Bishop*).
03062 The Last Rose of Summer (*Thomas Moore*).
03059 Robin Adair.
03061 Comin' thro' the Rye.
03054 Old Folks at Home.
03064 Within a Mile of Edinboro' Town.
03057 Kathleen Mavourneen (*Crouch*).
03060 Si vous n'avez rien a me dire (*Baroness Willy de Rothschild*).
03056 Jewel Song ("Faust "—*Gounod*).
03058 La Serenata (*Tosti*).
03055 Batti, Batti ("Don Giovanni"—*Mozart*).
03052 Pur Dicesti (*Lotti*).
03051 Voi che Sapete ("Nozze di Figaro"—*Mozart*).
03063 On Parting (*Adelina Patti*).

The Gramophone to-day is a musical instrument, and must be treated as such. Two kinds of Gramophone Needles are supplied. The ordinary Needle reproduces the voice with almost the same volume of sound as is given by the artiste when singing. The Pianissimo Gramophone Needle subdues the tones, and gives a very soft sweet effect, as of a voice heard in the distance. This Needle is suitable for playing the Gramophone in small rooms. It is also useful to the student, who may wish to repeat over and over again a phrase or a shake by Madame Patti, or a difficult piece of execution by that wonderful artiste, Mischa Elman. On no account should any but genuine Gramophone Needles be used with a Gramophone Record.

GRAMOPHONE, WITH OAK PEDESTAL

THE SHERATON GRAMOPH

"HIS MASTER'S VOICE"

On receipt of Postcard we will send Catalogues and Lists, also our brochures, "Opera at Home" and "The Living Voice," together with Name and Address of the nearest Dealer in our Goods.

TRADE MA

GRAMOPHONE

THE GRAMOPHONE & TYPEWRITER, Ltd., 21, CITY ROA LONDON, E.

costume, decor, and a first-rate orchestra, she was a pale reflection of her usual self, but there were others who found, often to the surprise of themselves and their sponsors, that their style was uniquely suited to this primitive instrument. One of these was Bert Sheppard who had little to offer an audience but a robust even tenor voice and good diction. He was used by the Gramophone Company as a general-purpose singer under a variety of names, and his repertoire included negro melodies, ballads, yodels, comic and patter songs. His greatest attribute was his spontaneous laugh, and his 'Laughing Song' and 'Whistling Coon' were world-famous. The 'Laughing Song' appealed particularly to the inhabitants of India, and half a million copies were sold there.

Another winner for the company was Ian Colquhoun (the 'Iron-Voiced Baritone'), who dressed in kilt and sang patriotic songs at the Alhambra. His rendering of 'The Absent-minded Beggar' was, for a live audience, nothing remarkable, but he made a name for himself by singing this on record. Nevertheless at the time of the Boer War he was eclipsed by what was little more than an effects record entitled 'The Departure of the Troopship', in which bugles sounded, voices were heard asking their loved ones to write, and troops sang 'Home, Sweet Home', which would seem to be the last possible song a soldier would bother with. It was said that it was this record that induced Melba (with tears in her eyes) to make gramophone records.

Because of the novelty, all gramophone music was popular, and operatic titbits, and their singers, became household names. Formerly the singers' public was restricted to the opera house or the concert hall, but when their voices were heard by the many, at exhibitions and promotion stunts, the artistes themselves became a national possession. Many of them took advantage of it, and regarded themselves as personalities and clowns. Caruso would fool about with stage business. In *Aida* he would tickle

Opposite: A 1906 advertisement for the Gramophone & Typewriter Ltd. Patti was well into her sixties and long past her best, and many buyers blamed the gramophone for what were really her singing deficiencies.
(The Bystander)

As the Edwardian age moved on, gramophones became cheaper, as this advertisement graphically reveals. (Woman's World)

a singer's nose with a chrysanthemum so that she sneezed, and in *La Bohème* he danced and grimaced and mimicked like a schoolboy. He was building up an image.

The profits of the Gramophone Company reflected the tremendous public interest: £79,348 in 1901, £137,268 in 1902, £252,285 in 1903. Other companies were entering the arena because of a loophole in the Berliner patent, but at the same time the phonograph companies were in deep water, and eventually in 1909 Edison closed down his phonograph works in Europe. He maintained that he had listened to thirty operas in their entirety, plus 140,000 songs, but this did not help him to stave off the collapse of cylinder music as opposed to disc music.

Zonophone was one of the rivals, but the Gramophone Company reacted by buying up the firm, taking over Zonophone's lucrative European business, running down its prestige records and using the label as an outlet for cheap discs. Zonophone's managing director started another company, the Odéon, which pioneered double-sided discs and recruited two best-selling singers, the versatile Lilli Lehmann and John McCormack. The Italian Fonotopia company confined its operations to the upper end of the market, but was never a real threat to the Gramophone Company.

Not surprisingly, there was a vocal minority that hated the gramophone. The Glasgow paper *The Baillie* declared in 1905 that 'gramophones and for that matter phonographs are the curse of this age and should be suppressed by statute, dynamite, or any other lethal weapon'. When one considers the low-price records that were being issued at that time, one cannot wonder. Florrie Forde was singing 'Jack, Jack, Jack', and Queenie Leighton was making a minor hit with 'The Crackling of the Pork'. Among the instrument curios was the banjo duet 'Navajo', described as an Indian two-step, a piccolo solo 'Patrole Comique', the 'Carnival of Venice' for saxophone solo, and a composition for cornet quartet with organ.

There were attempts to increase the playing time of a record. The maximum period was four minutes for a twelve-inch disc (this remained the barrier until the introduction of long-playing records after World War II). The firm of Neophone produced twenty-inch discs, plastic on cardboard, playing from eight to ten minutes, but this involved producing an instrument to play these monsters. Neophone could not cope with the double problem, the public did not seem overkeen, and the brave experiment faded after a few years, the company folding up in 1908.

Despite the claims made by gramophone propagandists, the first full-scale orchestral record had to wait until April 1909, when the London Palace orchestra recorded Tchaikovsky's *Nutcracker Suite*. The forty players were conducted by Hermann Finck, and it was said that the recording session occupied three whole days and cost the recording company £800. This record was made by the English branch of the Odéon company, now owned by the Carl Lindstrom Company of Germany which had swallowed most of the important European companies including Fonotopia and was a threat to the Gramophone Company's home market. Not that there was any chance of the Gramophone Company being assimilated; the plant in Hanover was fully occupied with producing discs for the German market, and there were other factories at Hayes in Middlesex, Riga (for Russia), Aussig (for Austria-Hungary), Ivry (for France), Barcelona (for Spain) and Calcutta for the previously undreamt-of Indian market.

The look of the records themselves had changed, the dog picture had been renamed 'His Master's Voice' and was now the recognised trade-mark in place of the angel with a quill. HMV, as the company was now known, seemed to be in an unassailable position, for a potential rival in Columbia had missed its chances and was mainly occupied with marketing American records. A new change of leadership occurred in 1909, and the Gramophone Company had to look to its laurels. Columbia was always at its elbow until 1931 when the two companies were amalgamated into EMI.

Honour was involved in producing reasonable-quality orchestral records, and when Odéon recorded Mendelssohn's *Midsummer Night's Dream* music, the Gramophone Company retaliated with Landon Ronald conducting with the New Symphony Orchestra half the first movement of Grieg's Piano Concerto with the young Backhaus as soloist. Columbia produced 'The Finest Orchestral Record Ever Issued'—Schubert's Eighth Symphony—and by the end of 1912 the gramophone companies' catalogues contained something of a smattering of orchestral music.

Orchestral music lacked the snob-appeal of the expensive operatic discs of a decade earlier, and because of the four-minute limit many music-lovers preferred to do without rather than listen to their masterpieces fragmented. It must be remembered that there was no instrument then in existence that could play long pieces of music in their entirety. The reproducing piano was well able to perform an adapted symphony in sections, which was perhaps the most musical way of presenting a great work. But the gramophone was the only means of even hinting a timbre.

The 1912 gramophone catalogues were still largely made up of the ephemeral and the trashy. The Gramophone Company claimed to have broken new ground with two Romances by Schumann for oboe solo, but otherwise there were such works as 'The Hairdresser' ('kept us in one long laugh' wrote the talking machine correspondent of the *Music Trades Record*), George Robey's 'Tempt Me Not', Harry Fragson ('the Caruso of the Halls') singing 'The Other Department Please', Harry Lauder doing 'The Blarney Stone', 'The Ghost of the Banjo Coon', a Sterndale-Bennett ballad 'Come to Town, Miss Brown', and an early essay in ragtime, 'That Hypnotising Man' by von Tilzer. There was also a dreadful comedy duet called 'A Sister to Assist 'Er' by Thomas le Breton, real name T. Murray Ford, author of 'The Confessions of Mrs May' and 'Jo Crupper, Bus Conductor'.

These records varied in price from 3s 6d to 5s 6d, but for 12s 6d one could have got the opera singer Tetrazzini on a twelve-inch pink label singing 'Home Sweet Home'. For this considerable sum of money, equivalent to £6 in our money, one could get what the trade press called 'individual touches, the suave cantabile, and the original finish to the shake'.

In February 1914 a milestone was reached when Arthur Nikisch and the Berlin Philharmonic Orchestra gathered before the recording trumpet and played Beethoven's Fifth Symphony. This was on four two-sided discs and sold in Germany for 48 marks (then £2 in English money), and there was great excitement in Britain as music-lovers waited for these discs, which reached them piecemeal, the last one arriving just before the war began. This, assuredly, thought the cognoscenti, was the quintessence of the recording art, and did not Nikisch himself say that the reproduction of instrumental music was absolutely true to nature from an artistic standpoint, 'and the sensation it produces is simply overpowering?'

Whether Nikisch, who had a world-wide reputation for his interpretation of Beethoven, was misquoted will never be known, but Toscanini commented on this recording in 1943 in no uncertain terms. Poor in sound and misrepresenting the conductor's artistry, the phrasing and spirit did not correspond to Toscanini's memories of Nikisch's performances. It is difficult to see how the German could have made a good job of it when one considers his orchestra for the occasion: six violins, two violas, and no drums or double basses.

Opera-lovers were far better served, with a complete *Trovatore* in 1906 recorded over a period of time and using sixteen different singers instead of the five principals stipulated by Verdi, a *Fledermaus* in 1907, and Gounod's *Faust* in 1908, while Pathé, the French company that had pioneered the phonograph in Europe but which had fallen behind on discs, used the chorus, orchestra, and leading singers of the Opéra-Comique for a number of operas including *Carmen*. Pathé also developed a twin-turntable

THE PHONOGRAPH CANNOT LIE.

German Dealer. "Now, mein Herr! You've chust heerd your lofely blaying rebroduced to berfection! Won't you buy one?"

Amateur Flautist. "Are you sure the thing's all right?"

German Dealer. "Zertainly, mein Herr."

Amateur Flautist. "Gad, then, if that's what my playing is like, I'm done with the flute for ever."

As with the camera, the phonograph was supposed not to lie. (Punch)

gramophone so that an opera could be presented with some attempt at continuity.

Classical titbits there were in some abundance, and provided that they carried a good tune and the orchestration was lucid there was a chance of them being acceptable to an undiscriminating audience. Violin solos came over well on record, and few of the great virtuosos of the time considered it beneath their dignity to play trivia—Kreisler even wrote his own, putting the blame on eighteenth-century composers. The gramophone did its part to make light classical music acceptable to the non-musical, a proselytiser like the barrel-piano, the disc musical box, the military and brass bands, and the hotel and seaside orchestras. Light music was not harmed by poor arrangements, though the deformed and truncated classical works must have made many initially receptive listeners wonder what all the fuss was about masterpieces. Schubert's Unfinished Symphony in eight minutes cannot have been convincing to anyone.

A fair amount of piano music was recorded in the Edwardian period, especially works such as the Chopin waltzes or mazurkas that could fit into four minutes, but piano music sounded far better on reproducing and player-pianos, and recording the fine pianists of the time was an act of duplication, for the reproducing piano, which electrically repeated a performance rather than a work, was in every way superior.

Until World War II the treasuries of music were looted for short works that would fill a record side or two sides, and this had the effect of introducing Mozart overtures to people who had never heard a Mozart symphony, and Beethoven's 'Fur Elise' to those who were not acquainted with Beethoven's piano sonatas (with the possible exception of the 'Moonlight', recorded as early as 1910 by Mark Hambourg). Certain pieces of music enjoyed an incredible vogue. Rachmaninoff's Prelude in C sharp minor was one of these, arranged for a variety of instruments including military band.

By far the most satisfactory items for a technician to deal with were talking pieces such as monologues, and comic songs, where diction was more important than musical shortcomings, and where the pleasure was intellectual rather than aesthetic. The gramophone was good at giving information, and in 1908 a spokesman of the Gramophone Company said that the company was going into the business of making records for political gatherings (short-lived aspirations but the idea was there). The folk song collectors found the gramophone a most useful research tool, and Bartok used it a good deal.

Not until electrical recording was evolved in the 1920s was there any serious attempt at reproduction fidelity, but by that time there was a major rival for the public's fickle hand—radio.

CHAPTER EIGHT

OUTDOOR MUSIC

THERE WERE SEVERAL kinds of outdoor music—that which one paid for, that which was free, and that for which one paid a bribe to have the music cut short. The Victorian streets resounded to the sound of music, and the Edwardian squares, terraces, rows, and roads inherited German bands, duos and trios playing every possible combination of instrument, barrel-organs and barrel-pianos, hawkers making noises that could only marginally be called music, and genuine musicians who had struck hard times

NOCTURNE IN THE OLD KENT ROAD

The Edwardians experienced every conceivable combination of instruments in their waking moments, and harp and cornet in duet no doubt had their supporters. (Punch)

146

This illustration to a story by W. W. Jacobs shows that the barrel-piano was still a feature of the London scene, though it largely died out between the wars. (Strand)

and were eking out coppers received through charity with *ad hoc* performances. The Edwardians did not have anything so pervasive as the transistor radio to contend with, and a shopper would not have to face up to piped music but only Palm Court orchestras in the prestige stores. The Edwardians were also too early for that outdoor peril of the 1920s and 1930s, the ex-serviceman pushing a wind-up gramophone in a perambulator.

The barrel-piano, variously called the cylinder piano, the street piano, the piano organ, and the grinder organ, was invented in the early years of the nineteenth century by Joseph Hicks of Bristol, and was developed throughout the Victorian period. Usually hand-cranked, a clockwork piano was introduced in 1884, and proved a great favourite; some versions had tuned bells and a drum.

The Italians were involved both in the manufacture of barrel-pianos and in their exploitation, and there was a lively trade in their hire (with or without monkeys) from depositories in Clerkenwell, an area in which two of the leading makers, Joseph Piana Canova and Luigi Villa, set up in business. For those who hated the barrel-piano, and the insouciance of their operators who would not take no for an answer, a fresh refinement was introduced in 1910, a type of machine known as the zither-banjo which was so loud that it was asserted that it could be heard a mile away.

Another development of the barrel-piano was the book-music

Although this photograph was taken in the 1920s *it represents a common Edwardian scene. Hawkers and buskers would play anything that they could get their hands on.* (Wonderful London)

piano, in which a punched cardboard strip, folded for convenience into squares, replaced the pinned barrel, but although this meant that the repertoire could be changed the operators were not too keen on it, for the music books tore, got lost, and were not so hardy as the barrels. Nor was it financially advantageous for the operator to change his repertoire, for that would have removed part of the threat. His aim was to clobber the listener with the same old tune played over and over again.

Barrel-organs (erroneously regarded as synonymous with the barrel-piano) were less widely used, and the hurdy-gurdy was a fairly rare instrument. It had a rather agreeable nasal whine, and little carrying power.

Hawkers and buskers played anything that they could lay their hands on. The cornet à piston was a favourite instrument, and with the vogue for brass bands there were usually numbers of second-hand instruments on the market. The cornet, with its penetrating, rather coarse tone, was highly favoured by the street bands.

The buskers often operated in twos, one singing, the other accompanying, a popular instrument being the concertina, a chord-producing keyboardless device that was easy to learn. The vogue for musical comedy, the sudden upsurge of the cinema, and the vast audiences that could be accommodated in the music halls run by the syndicates meant that buskers had a captive audience in cinema, music hall, and theatre queues, and a public that could not go away was manna to the performers. Whereas it was claimed that the mechanical organs and pianos penetrated into the remotest slums and alleys and spread musical culture among the dregs of the people, there were few who would defend the buskers, a race entirely distinct from the members of the German bands who were customarily expert musicians.

Outdoor music of all kinds was rarely accepted whole-heartedly, though Parliamentary Bills had done something to remedy some of the worst abuses. By the time the Edwardian period arrived it was accepted that it was the proper and humane thing to provide music in the parks, and the days had gone when it was feared that a crowd of people gathered together in a public place was bound to erupt in violence. The only question that arose relating to bands in the parks, and other forms of municipal open-air music, was how much money should be allotted to them out of the rates, and this varied enormously from town to town.

The opening of band-stands was a popular activity of urban councils during the Edwardian period. The illustration shows the opening of the new bandstand at New-ton Abbot, Devon.

There were some councils that thought they had a duty to provide the best kind of music for the poor, and made an effort to include in their band programmes the acknowledged masterpieces of the past. The Parks and Open Spaces Commission of the London County Council spent £12,500 a year on their one orchestra and two military bands. The London County Council could depend on a pool of more than 100 players, but they drew the line at performances in winter, unlike Sheffield which provided music all the year round.

The London County Council bands were not expected to supply all the open-air music, and over a year as many as ninety outside bands were employed. London felt that it had an educational responsibility towards the people, and in 1907 a London County Council spokesman said:

> It would be utterly absurd to force down high class programmes where the public do not want them. To a certain extent we are bound to suit the public taste: we don't want to be told that the whole programme is above their heads. But on the other hand it is our duty to try to raise the public taste.

To judge by their programmes, the council did this admirably. In a series of six band concerts were included Beethoven's Fourth Symphony, Raff's Third Symphony (which has probably not been heard since), Schumann's Fourth and Tchaikovsky's Sixth, plus overtures by Smetana, Weber, Brahms, and Sullivan.

Leeds established band concerts in 1903, playing in winter to audiences of 2,500 at charges of between 2d and 1s 6d. By 1909 audiences had shrunk to 1,300, and admission fees were put up to between 6d and 3s. Sheffield provided bands in the park but no money, and with reserved seats at 1d and 3d they faced a deficit of £1,200, made up by taking from the rates income an eighth of a penny in the pound (raising £700) while the Tramways Committee donated £500. In 1908 Manchester provided for its inhabitants more than 500 band performances at a cost of £3,000, obtained from the rates, and it was reckoned that 2,600,000 people had attended these concerts.

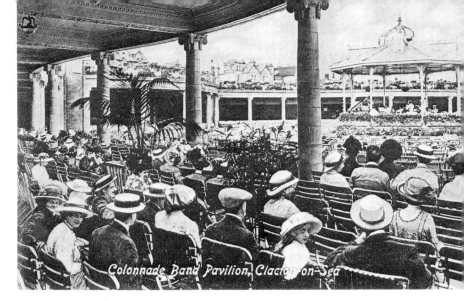

Seaside music was an important part of Edwardian leisure, and every fashionable resort had its band pavilion. This photograph depicts the pavilion at Clacton-on-Sea.

Perhaps the most adventurous of the towns and cities was Bournemouth, which formed its municipal band in 1893, and in 1895 began giving classical concerts, admission a shilling. Bournemouth music centred around the Godfrey dynasty. Dan Godfrey (Sir Dan in 1922) was director at Bournemouth from 1893 to 1925; his father, also Dan, was a prolific composer of dance music and bandmaster of the Grenadier Guards, while *his* father, Charles, had been bandmaster of the Coldstream Guards. By 1911 Dan Godfrey had conducted nearly 1,000 symphony concerts, and almost single-handed he demonstrated that provincial music-making could be accomplished at a high level.

Seaside music was an important part of Edwardian lesiure. Every fashionable resort had its band, and some of them, including Eastbourne, made considerable profits. Musical comedy had given Britain a corpus of work that was widely appreciated by poor and rich; the lush songs from *The Merry Widow* went down as well in Blackpool as they did in Torquay. Because musical-comedy tunes were shapely and good, they could be adapted for almost any combination, from indifferent hotel orchestras peeping from behind their potted palms to the wholly

There was a good deal of inter-regimental rivalry regarding military bands, who were encouraged to show off their paces to the general public. (Punch)

professional military bands, which were encouraged to show themselves at seaside resorts. As early as 1871 the bands of the Royal Artillery and Grenadier Guards had augmented London Promenade Concerts, and there was a good deal of inter-regimental rivalry as to which had the best band. Just as Bournemouth had provided a lead in municipal music, so in 1876 the town had a military band of sixteen players, all of whom had been in the Italian army and wore that uniform.

The military bandsmen were technically as good as any civilian musicians, and were keen to show off their prowess to the general public. In 1907 the band of the Coldstream Guards had played at the Dublin Festival to an audience of 15,000, and had included in their repertoire a formidable arrangement of Bach's Organ Fantasia and Fugue in G minor. They were often compared in a casual manner with brass bands, but there were few brass bandsmen who would have taken on their military counterparts.

Less often seen at the seaside, more often at naval stations such as Devonport and Portsmouth, were the bands of the Royal Navy. The Navy was much later in the field, and it was not until 1903 that the Royal Naval School of Music was inaugurated. Between 1903 and 1908 the school turned out 1,200 trained men and boys, and by the latter date there were in existence fifty-three bands (playing strength eleven to twenty-four). These were principally sea-going bands, and the public had little chance of comparing them with their military counterparts. Indeed, the military bands existed in a world of their own, unaffected by trends and current fashions, and the only combination with which they could be compared was the military band of the American march king, Sousa, who toured Britain in 1900–5.

Another important element in seaside music were the pierrots and others of that ilk. A pierrot is defined in *Chambers Twentieth Century Dictionary* as a buffoon with loose long-sleeved white robe, and was recognisably a figure from the *commedia dell' arte*, a type of character often painted by the French court painters, and there is no rhyme or reason why the species suddenly appeared on the seaside sands, replacing, without much effort, their predecessors the nigger minstrels. Pierrots did answer a demand for more sophisticated entertainment than Bones and Mr Interlocutor,

Musical-comedy songs were widely disseminated by the gramophone, in sheet-music form, and by seaside pierrot troupes.

Sandown in the Isle of Wight was an early venue for the pierrot.

but it appears to have been a matter of chance that the performers chose that particular costume.

An exceptionally gifted nigger minstrel troupe, such as the one that existed at Llandudno, was able to fight off the threat of the pierrot, but most found that it was better to join them than fight them, and so scrubbed off their black make-up and applied for membership. Entrepreneurs realised that there was real money to be made from the new craze, and hired pitches from the councils. Scarborough, for example, charged £600 for a season, the corporation guaranteeing that that one particular troupe or combination would be free from competition. Such sums of money could be found only by backers, rarely by troupes.

Some resorts erected pavilions and engaged troupes on a percentage basis, the members often recruited from musical-comedy companies between tours, but the better troupes were those who had been together for some time and had worked out a coherent programme. One of the best-known of these troupes was 'The Follies', dreamed up by H. G. Pelissier after he had seen a troupe at Sandown in the Isle of Wight. Pierrots had graduated to pier and pavilion from houseboat and yacht, and 'The Marguerites' had been one of the first groups to wear masks for its entertainment about 1890. A year later the first pierrots arrived, with harmonium, banjo, a comedian and a singer.

'The Follies' made their first professional appearance on Worthing Pier in 1897, and they were emulated by other troupes such as 'The Aristocrats', 'The Beaux and Belles', 'The Brownies',

'Charivari', 'The White Coons', 'The Cigarettes', 'The Gaieties', and 'The Antiques'. Many artistes of the future were nurtured in these shows—Fay Compton was one of the soubrettes in 'The Follies'.

At first, as Pelissier admitted, he found the public unresponsive, and recalled an old lady at a thin house saying, 'Ah, well! they all look very happy—poor things!' Pierrots and pierrettes were the old travelling players brought up to date; they had to be versatile, turning their hand to anything, and in the lesser troupes the masculine lead had to take his turn to 'bottle' (go round with the hat). Unquestionably the standard of some of the shows the pierrots put on was atrocious, and 'The Follies' themselves were not free from blame, with excruciatingly bad parodies and take-offs of music hall and well-known shows. Pelissier, who died in 1913 at the age of thirty-nine, was a bluff tubby man, composer, singer, and actor, and as his talent was minor anyway, it is not surprising that his work-rate was more commendable than the quality of his acts. His songs were no better than thousands of other drawing-room ballads of the period (they included 'Awake', 'I Want Somebody to Love Me', 'In My Garden of Roses', and 'Oh, What a Happy Land Is England)'.

Most pierrot troupes had their tales of how, to get new material without paying for it, they went to the music halls to take down the words of the latest ditty, how, out of season, they left the familiar purlieus of Margate and Scarborough and worked the Boat Race, the Derby, and Henley Regatta, and during the season making up their money by selling songs and photographs or doing Punch-and-Judy shows. Mr Will Tyrrell of the Royal Ramsgate Minstrels recalled the days in the nineties when nigger minstrels had to turn overnight into pierrots to remain commercially viable, and this meant that their repertoire was obsolete. He was contemptuous of the law of copyright as it applied to open-air singing: 'there is as good as none, for all you have to do is to leave off singing when you are asked'.

On the economics of running a troupe, 'the sketches draw the biggest crowd, but the songs draw the most money'. The hazards: the sea coming in and washing the properties into the sea. 'Once,' said Tyrrell, 'during a song the piano accompaniment stopped

All pierrot troupes had their tales of woe—pianos washed out to sea, tents collapsing, and unresponsive audiences demanding impossibilities (such as quality).
(Strand)

dead, and the crowd began to shriek with laughter. I looked round—the pianist had disappeared. The stool had been washed from under him, and he had gone clean over on his back.' The piano itself was very vulnerable, and was kept swathed in flannel to stop the damp getting at the wires and rusting them. An unexpected rain shower could cause the keys to swell and stick together. Asked what happened then, the pianist of the Royal Margate Minstrels replied, 'Well, we just give the audience a taste of caterwauling, and then, explaining that the piano has had a sudden attack of sea-sickness we whistle our accompaniments.'

If pierrot shows were compared to their advantage with nigger minstrels, so were they in their turn rated against the revues that preceded World War I. There was much in common, and also at times the programmes of 'The Follies' had an almost uncanny resemblance to those of the early Victorian burlesques. It is interesting to compare an early parody of *Hamlet* with Pelissier's:

A hero's life I'll sing, his story shall my pen mark;
He was not the King, but 'Amlet, Prince of Denmark.

His mammy, she was young, the crown she'd set her eyes on;
Her husband stopped her tongue; she stopped his ears with
  pison.

That was Sam Cowell's version, sung in Evans's, the song and
supper rooms in Covent Garden. And here is Pelissier's:

No wonder that I'm called the moody Dane
When my uncle with the State plays fast and loose;
For it's quite enough to drive a prince insane
When he sees his country going to the deuce.

How flat this is compared with the dash and vigour of the
Victorian version of more than half a century earlier! And one
sees this humdrum quality throughout pierrot productions.
Pelissier saw himself and his company as forces to be reckoned
with:

As for 'The Follies', the principal *role* they fill in the scheme
of twentieth-century society is satire. I do not propose in this
article [in the *Strand Magazine* 1909] to compare myself with
Juvenal . . .

An absolutely uncritical audience induces complacency, and

*Pierrots fluctuated un-
easily between profes-
sional and amateur
status. Some troupes
were good, some were
bad, and some were
awful.*

where there is no rival entertainment, anything suffices. Pelissier told one or two stories against his company and its failure to communicate with its audience. A burlesque pantomine was performed:

> Everything was caricatured, and we fondly imagined that the audience was ill with excess of mirth. One sweet old soul was asked how she liked the pantomime. 'Really,' she said, 'I've no doubt they did their best—but people could not help laughing. I don't know when I've seen such a disgraceful pantomime—the scenery was wretched and the dresses tawdry. The only pretty song was "Dear Heart"; but there was so much noise going on behind the scenes that I could scarcely hear a word'.

'The Follies' took great comfort by an appearance with Albert Chevalier at the Queen's Hall, music hall dates, and a Royal Command to Sandringham, where Edward VII laughed

Pierrots obtained good publicity by an appearance with Albert Chevalier at the Queen's Hall and a Royal Command to Sandringham. A pierrot could even figure as hero in popular women's fiction. (Woman's World)

uproariously at a take-off of Wagnerian opera. In essence 'The Follies' were an ordinary burlesque troupe using an outdoor environment on pier and beach, getting over difficulties through good humour and perpetuating the hoary theatrical legend of 'the show must go on'.

'The Follies' had a good resident comic writer, Arthur Wimperis, who managed to pep up the pedestrianism of H. G. Pelissier's contributions, and who spent an inordinate amount of time making the programme notes amusing: 'An egg-proof curtain will be lowered at least once during the performance for the protection of artists'. Wimperis made a speciality of comic 'advertisements':

Pears' whisky brightens the complexion
Dewar's soap for the gullet (won't wash clothes)
The Phit-eesi chair
Gun's 3/9 hats

To give an idea of pierrot humour, here is part of the 'cast list' of Pelissier's *Everybody's Benefit*:

1. Signor Caroozo (by kind permission of the Gramophone Company).
2. Mr Arthur Bradsmith and Chorus, from the *Gay Gazeekas* in his celebrated song, 'I want to be a Hero' (by kind permission of the audience).
3. The Supper Scene from *The School for Scandal*. Played entirely by Leading Actor Managers (by kind permission of each other).

Pierrot troupes gave the thumbs-up to amateur theatricals and bands of mediocre semi-professionals who did shows for garden parties, but the success of 'The Follies' did encourage four Cambridge undergraduates to form an entertainment called 'The March Hares'. The 'band' of this troupe was Philip Braham (composer of 'Limehouse Blues') who played piano, cymbals, drums, celesta, and triangle. Eventually 'The March Hares' led after the war into 'The Co-optimists' which became a cult.

Music publishers saw the sales possibilities in pierrot troupes, and sponsored concert parties just as they backed ballad concerts. Among the pierrot songs were 'Two Little Dover Soles', 'A Single Cingalee', 'Come Roller Skating', and 'Mr Jolly Boy'. Some were poor even by seaside standards, and Pelissier's 'The Sun Song' was reviewed in 1913 in ironical terms: it 'depends for its meaning entirely upon a wet summer. Its usefulness is therefore limited'.

It was a far step from the amateurism and cliquishness of the pierrot troupes with their own slang to the dedicated single-mindedness of the brass bands. The brass-band movement had more in common with the amateur choirs than with other forms of music-making; the bands thrived on competition, and although the 1890s were their golden years, enthusiasm persisted throughout the Edwardian period. In 1889 there were reckoned to be 40,000 amateur brass bands in the country, predominantly in the midlands and the north of England, and one firm of musical instrument makers had 10,000 brass bands on its books. In addition, the Salvation Army had upwards of 1,000 brass bands.

There was a move in 1900 to try to strengthen the brass-band

'By the sea! By the sea! The beautiful silvery sea! Where you hear the brass band play "Yip-i-addy-i-ay-i-ay" . . .'

"BY THE SEA".

By the sea! By the sea!
The beautiful silvery sea!
Where you hear the brass band play;
' Yip-i-addy-i-ay-i-ay!",
With your girlie—girlie,
That's where you want to be,
Down on the sands, the silvery sands,
By the side of the silvery sea!

Songs of the Season

By the turn of the century, the Salvation Army had upwards of a thousand brass bands, and many fine musicians emerged from their alfresco performances. (Around London)

movement in the south of England, and a series of Crystal Palace concerts, later known as the National Brass Band Festival, was started. The number of bands taking part went up from 29 in 1900 to 117 in 1903; 1903 brought a truly outstanding player to the notice of the public—W. Paris Chambers, who could encompass four octaves on his cornet (the usual range is two octaves).

British brass bands began to enjoy international fame and in 1905 the famous 'Besses o' the Barn' band went to Paris. In 1906 the Black Dyke Mills band went to America and received a tremendous ovation. Many well-known composers, including Elgar and Granville Bantock, began writing music especially for a brass combination, and this caused musical snobs to re-evaluate brass bands, commonly supposed to contain only illiterate miners and factory workers and worthy of playing merely flashy fantasies and medleys (such as *Gems of Mendelssohn*, the test piece at the Crystal Palace in 1904).

By 1908 there were five graded contests, including reed bands, boys' bands, and, somewhat oddly, concertina bands, and 165 bands competed, most of them from Yorkshire and Lancashire. Despite the efforts of J. Henry Iles, the prime mover in bringing

The Crystal Palace remained a bastion of music-making, amateur and professional. (Around London)

brass-band contests south from their traditional venue, Belle Vue, Manchester, brass bands had not caught on in the south, despite the enthusiasm of large audiences (60,000 at the Crystal Palace in 1908).

There is no greater monument to do-it-yourself music than the success of the brass-band movement. Much of it was due to an alliance between capital (which supplied the money for instruments and allowed employees to take time off to practice) and labour (which supplied the men). Some employers feared that brass bands would be used against them, for leading marching strikers, and although this inevitably happened, unquestionably the social good that the band movement accomplished more than outweighed this. It was a pioneer in grass-roots popular music, urban and unselfconscious, and not until after World War II was other working-class participation in music-making a viable proposition.

CHAPTER NINE

THE CHORAL TRADITION

BY THE END of the nineteenth century, some of the outstanding Victorian choral societies had gone under. These included the Sacred Harmonic Society (1832–89), which had had its home at Exeter Hall from 1834 to 1880 and which was then ejected by the new purchasers, the YMCA, on the ground that 'oratorios for amusement' were improper. There was also the Choral Harmonists' Society (1833–52), H. D. Leslie's Choir (1855–87), a fine, highly trained, hand-picked ensemble, Joseph Barnby's various choral activities from 1867 to 1896, Novello's Oratorio Concerts (1885–9), and Willing's Choir (1889–92). But there were many London choral societies that carried on, and new ones were formed throughout the Edwardian period, the most important being the London Choral Society (1903), the Novello Choir (1905), Edward Mason's Choir (1909) and the London County Council Choral Unions (1909). And these were just in London. For many people choirs did not even begin until one reached north of Birmingham.

Choirs that did suffer during the first years of the twentieth century were London suburban societies. Up to about 1895 almost every district, rich and poor, had some kind of choral society, and a visitor to London could go to a different choral concert every night of the week without leaving the south bank of the Thames. With the increasing efficiency of public transport, there was no longer any need for a suburbanite to have to find

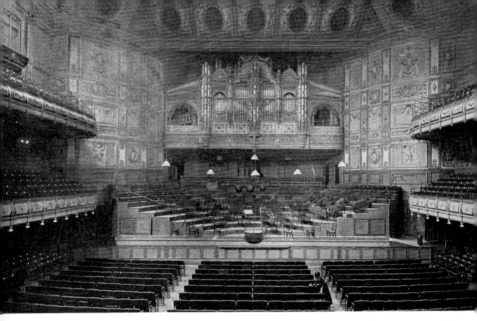

Henry J. Wood, conductor of the promenade concerts at the Queen's Hall, announced his intention of forming a select choir of 1,000 voices, but nothing came of this despite the excellent facilities at the Queen's Hall. (Around London)

his amusement in the vicinity of his home, and the upsurge in bicycle travel gave all but the very poor personalised transport. The coming of the electric tram and the first Underground railways dealt a death-blow to suburban music making. If music lovers wanted to hear good choirs they went into town, and the more adventurous singers were inclined to prefer the prestigious centralised choirs rather than the patchwork affair run by perhaps an elderly clergyman in a decrepit church hall two streets away.

Even in conditions that one would have thought alien to the success of something so ostensibly outdated as choral work, there were men who worked hard to present sacred and secular music as competently as they knew how. Henry J. Wood, who had been conductor of the Promenade Concerts at the Queen's Hall since 1895, announced his intention of forming a select choir of 100 voices—'a truly representative choir, trained with high aims and endued it possible with an enthusiasm and an *esprit de corps* that will gain for it a permanent usefulness to music in that special branch of the art to which its energies will be devoted'. Nothing came of this bold venture, nor of Mr Wood's Orchestral Society proposed a year later, but down in Dulwich, Arthur Fagge was more energetic. In 1903 Weingartner had been appointed to perform Beethoven's Ninth Symphony, and looked round for a chorus to participate in the last movement. He failed to find one in central London, but the Dulwich Choral Society rose to the occasion and officiated. The press were enthusiastic, and Mr Fagge planned the formation of the London Choral Society.

The Musical Times looked on the project with approval:

> We understand he has had shoals of applications for performing membership, but so high—and rightly so—is the standard of voice and reading power which has been set up that the full complement of 300 first-rate singers has not yet been reached.

Fagge was determined not to rely on the old war-horses, the oratorios *The Messiah* and *Elijah*, and one of the first works put into rehearsal was Elgar's *Dream of Gerontius*, then considered very advanced. Fagge continued the policy of promoting new works, and his choir gave the first performance of Bantock's *Omar Khayyam*, luscious Eastern confectionery but more demanding than the oratorios of the nineteenth century. One of Fagge's problems was that it was easy enough to find good women singers, but males, especially tenors, were hard to come by; it was a problem that he shared with other choirmasters.

The music firm of Novello started a choir among its own staff in 1905, and a large number of organisations were involved in running their own choirs, including the Baltic Exchange, the Great Western and Great Eastern Railways, the Stock Exchange, the insurance companies, and banks, while the Civil Service had two choirs. There is no question that their efforts come under the heading of popular music; they enjoyed singing, and for the participants that was an end to it so far as they were concerned. When present-day musicologists look askance at the run-of-the-mill works toeing the line between the sacred and the secular, what might be termed oratorios for agnostics, it is wise to remember what the market was—amateur choirs which liked the novel but not necessarily the new, which enjoyed a challenge, but a challenge within a circumscribed formula. It is then easy enough to understand the appeal of, for example, Bantock's choral works and the incredibly popular *Hiawatha's Wedding Feast* by Coleridge-Taylor.

Singing for pleasure without thought of monetary recompense was also pursued by the London County Council's choral unions, the members of which had graduated from the council's evening classes in singing (the unions in the title are London districts). They were good enough to do *The Messiah* at the Queen's Hall before a critical concert audience, and also gave MacCunn's *Wreck of the Hesperus* an outing. The cellist Edward Mason formed a choir specifically for the purpose of singing new works by young composers, and was adventurous enough to do works by Bax and Delius. Unfortunately Mason was killed in World War I and there was no one to carry on his commendable work.

Nevertheless choral music never caught on in the south as it did in the north, and the spirit of competition that spurred on the northern choirs was lacking. The competition festival movement had grown swiftly since it had been started in Westmorland in 1885, and although this movement was primarily for the benefit of villagers and dwellers in small towns, it also encompassed the singers of those cities with a long choral tradition who were eager to try their mettle against all comers. Competition was as stern and trenchant as in brass-band contests.

Huddersfield had had a choral society since 1836, Bradford's Old Choral Society was founded in 1821 (with 300 voices even then), Warrington had had a choir since 1834, Oldham since 1846, and although the Manchester Vocal Society did not come into existence until 1866 it had something unique about it— it never appeared in public with a conductor, even when the work to be performed was in forty parts. The industrial midlands also had long traditions. The Birmingham choir was singing from 1855, and the Nottingham Sacred Harmonic Society was inaugurated in 1846. Not surprisingly, the stalwarts of these

The Albert Hall was never fully utilised for choral music despite its capacity and suitability. Many northern choirs envied Londoners this fine building. (Around London)

organisations did not drop their music scores when the monarch changed, and, indeed, in Sheffield it seemed that the choral life of the city was to take on a new lease when the energetic Henry Coward arrived on the scene, a passionate believer in getting the utmost out of a choir. He developed a technique of his own which he called 'large-scaled open tone', and which his detractors called merely loud. Throughout the Edwardian period Coward took over conductorships in the north as they fell vacant, travelling relentlessly between Sheffield, Huddersfield, Barnsley, Preston, Newcastle-on-Tyne, and Derby, firing his choirs with his own enthusiasm. If they could not sing better than the much-despised choirs of the effete south, they could certainly sing louder (though in 1911 Henry Wood undertook to train the Sheffield Festival, cut down the volume and increased tonal colour).

In 1905 a writer in the *Musical Times* wrote a glowing eulogy of northern choirs, quoting Elgar's words that 'the true musical centre of England is not to be sought in London but much further north', and continuing:

I have heard choirs of mill-girls that made me wonder what

Suburban music-making went into decline with the great advances in public transport. Why go to hear a semi-professional concert in Streatham when an electric tramcar could whisk one to a 'real' concert in the West End? (Wonderful London)

was left for the archangels; I have heard choirs of rough men brought to the fine edge of a solo quartet of trombones, but that crowning glory of the North, the well-selected mixed choir carefully trained by some local conductor, can touch the heart and compel the unwilling tear in a way that nothing else can.

Unquestionably many of the circumstances that caused the decline of London suburban choral singing occurred in the north. Public transport, too, was making parochialism antiquated, and the tentacles of mass entertainment represented by the Hippo-dromes and Empires of the music-hall tycoons were depriving choirs of their male singers. Towns such as Huddersfield and Leeds which were, when their choirs were started, small towns surrounded by miles of unspoiled countryside, were rapidly losing their distinctive flavour as industrial town was joined to industrial town by ribbon-building until it was difficult for even a native to know where one town ended and another began.

There were other factors. The old school of singers, happy to bellow their heads off in the service of Handel, were worried by the amount of meddling that was going on with the traditional

favourites. Henry J. Wood, not renowned for his fidelity to the
score, had made a *Messiah* omelette, speeding up and slowing
down, and bombarding a Birmingham audience with frenetic
Hallelujahs. Not content with this he completely rescored the
work to satisfy contemporary demands (he also did this with
Handel's other oratorios and over sixty Bach cantatas). An old-
established baritone did not like this kind of thing, and just as
reprehensible was the act of stripping from the venerable trunk
the bark of countless rattling good performances. At the turn of
the century, Edward Bridge, a somewhat dim establishment
composer who was for thirty-six years organist of Westminster
Abbey, announced that he proposed to print a purified score of
The Messiah, having gone back to the original manuscript and
knowing what Handel intended; he therefore inserted an organ
for accompanying recitative where Handel had specified a
harpsichord, and for Albert Hall performances he specified an
orchestra of 100 and a choir of 800. As in Handel's day the instrumentalists outnumbered the choir, this could hardly be called a
constructive re-evaluation, though the Bridge version was used
at the Albert Hall until 1922.

Without realising it, Bridge was doing precisely what north-
country singers would have wanted—encouraging them to
scream their heads off—but other academics were more
scrupulous, or so it seemed. Prout promised that 'the excrescence
of additional accompaniments' should be removed, but only
'so far as feasible under modern conditions of performance'.
The work of Bridge and Prout and the others gave conductors a
free hand to pep up or restyle *The Messiah* just as they wished,
and not surprisingly many choirs resented the liberties that were
taken with their beloved war-horse.

Amateur choirs were also suspicious of the new works that
were being put on the market, and northerners did not have the
southern zeal for the new. Many had learned their singing under
the Tonic Sol-fa method, excellent for straightforward works of
the past but almost useless in dealing with music that was even
slightly chromatic, and confronted by Rutland Boughton's
Midnight (Birmingham, 1909), Havergal Brian's *By the Waters of
Babylon* (Liverpool, 1909), Vaughan Williams's *Towards the*

Unknown Region (Leeds, 1907), or Granville Bantock's *Atlanta in Calydon* (Manchester, 1912), they looked back longingly at the simple and simple-minded oratorios and cantatas that had once been performed so frequently and were now gathering dust— Alfred Gaul's *The Holy City* (1882), for example, a cantata that had sold 162,000 copies by 1914.

It was difficult to feel competitive when the new works edged into the repertoire, often with a bit of discreet bribery by publishers, were not worth making an effort for, and with rehashed *Messiah*s it needed a choirmaster with the dynamism of Coward to prevent enthusiasm seeping away. The great choral tradition of the north was oiled by enthusiasm, not technique, and in an atmosphere of social and musical insecurity, some of the steam went out of it.

CHAPTER TEN

FOLK MUSIC—
THE REVIVAL THAT FAILED

In 1851 there died at the age of ninety-four one of the earliest collectors of authentic folk tunes, George Thomson, an amateur musician of Edinburgh. He went into the Scottish countryside, gathering Scottish tunes and publishing them with verses by Burns and Walter Scott and accompaniments written, at his request, by Haydn and Beethoven. Thomson also garnished Irish and Welsh airs, but totally ignored English folk song—so far as he was concerned, there was no such animal. This attitude towards the incredible corpus of English folk music took a long time to be dissipated.

Between 1838 and 1840 William Chappell had issued his *Collection of National English Airs*, followed twenty years later by *Popular Music of the Olden Time*, and it was Chappell who founded the Musical Antiquarian Society. There was some confusion in Chappell's mind between folk music and art music, for it was widely held at the time that folk music was a bastard relation and that the way to rehabilitate it was to tidy it up, formalise it, and place it in its setting. Folk music was quaint and amusing, but not to be compared in respectability with madrigals, in which Chappell was very interested.

Chappell was an antiquary, not a field worker, but the work he did was valuable, and for a long time he was a lone figure, appreciated mainly by ballad composers who browsed through his collections looking for something that they could further emasculate. In 1893 a new edition of *Popular Music of the Olden Time* was published, and encouraged others to carry on his work.

The 1880s saw the first signs that English musicians were becoming aware of their heritage. In 1889 Lucy Broadwood reissued a small collection of Sussex and Surrey folk songs (with additions) that her uncle had brought out in 1843, William Alexander Barrett published *English Folk-Songs* in 1891, and the Reverend S. Baring-Gould, composer of 'Onward Christian Soldiers', put out, in association with the Rev H. Fleetwood Sheppard, *Songs of the West*. Frank Kidson of Leeds published two volumes in the 1890s, *English Peasant Songs* and *Songs of the North Countrie* (publishers liked olde-worlde touches).

It was difficult for collectors to put down the songs as they heard them; instinctively they modernised them for a genteel audience, and there were few with the objectivity of John Broadwood, the man who had made his collection of sixteen songs in 1843, who, when an organist insisted on harmonising them to suit convention, stuck to his guns and said 'Musically it may be wrong, but I will have it exactly as my singers sang it.'

A leading figure in the late Victorian search for folk song was the musicologist J. A. Fuller-Maitland, who was also heavily involved in the resurrection of Tudor and Stuart art music. With Lucy Broadwood he brought out one of the most influential collections, *English County Songs* (1893).

By the end of the century it was realised that England had a repository of folk melody that was second to none, and even the musical journals were sitting up and taking notice, inviting readers to send in folk tunes to their editors. The *Musical Times* was one of these periodicals:

> In many cases the songs have been preserved by tradition, the son singing the song for the performance of which his father before him was famous. These ditties were at all times difficult to collect, as they were only heard at rustic gatherings, harvest homes, sheep-shearings, and Christmas revels. Now that the rustic mind delights in parading the flaunting shoddy of the music-hall in preference to its own sub-

stantial if less gaudy homespun, the difficulties are increased. It is impossible, therefore, unaided, for one collector to gather together materials that have yet some existence though they are widely scattered.

True, but there were dozens of collectors of varying capabilities scouring the countryside in carriage, by train, and on horseback. There were the scrupulous disciples of Mr Broadwood, and there were the revisers, considering that the ignorant peasants were getting the music all wrong and that the words were so shocking that they could not possibly be written down for a polite public. Baring-Gould was distressed by the words of 'Strawberry Fair' and rewrote them. There was no doubt about it; the rude rustics were rude indeed, and liked their dirty songs.

Unquestionably it was difficult work, for collectors had not only to contend with art songs of perhaps fifty years earlier posing as folk songs, but also 'folk songs' published by the London broadside printers, dreamed up by a street-hawker with a violin in the squalid alleys of Seven Dials.

It all needed a co-ordinator, and in 1898 the Folk Song Society was founded, with 110 members, including leading establishment composers of the time such as Stainer, Stanford, Mackenzie and Parry, musical journalists, singers, and literary men. In 1904 Ralph Vaughan Williams and Cecil Sharp joined the committee. Sharp was the dynamo of the Folk Song Society, fierce, single-minded, immensely energetic (he collected 3,000 songs in England), a missionary willing to overthrow all the heresies he could find (and these included the classical masters of the past). By the time the Edwardian age began, the folk revival was ready to blossom.

Sharp did not suffer fools gladly. In one of his lectures he claimed that the melodies of Beethoven and Schubert were scarcely to be mentioned in the same breath with the songs of Somerset, and, as Vaughan Williams wrote, 'With Sharp it was a case of "Under which king, Bezonian? Speak or die." ' He added that 'you had to be either pro-folk-song or anti-folk-song, and I came down heavily on the folk-song side'. Sharp broke with the Victorian conception of folk-song collecting as an agreeable pursuit for country vicars; he was determined to make folk music a dominant feature of contemporary popular music, and drew a distinction between folk music and the popular music of the music hall and the shop ballad. Folk music grew, ordinary popular music was composed. Sir Hubert Parry was at one with him, consumed with a bitter hatred of modern popular song, which he associated with jerry-building, shoddy clothes, sham jewellery and fish shops. Folk song 'grew in the heart of the people before they devoted themselves so assiduously to the making of quick returns'.

In 1906 Cecil Sharp gave an important lecture. It was reported in the *Musical Times*:

> In the *Journal of the Folk-Song Society* several variants heard of the same song are printed, and the lecturer boldly applies the doctrines of evolution to explain the adoption of final forms (if there are any). He thinks that many of the existing tunes began with mere inflection, and that, gradually, in the course of generations, they have assumed their existing form. So we have geometrical increase, constant variation, struggles for existence, and survival of the fittest—the communally made tune, embodying the rhythmic and tonal likings of the race and district.

For many of the members of the Folk Song Society, Sharp was going too far, and many of the composers who had joined the society at its outset, and who had used folk song as a starting-point for their own works, resented Sharp's purism. In the same year as this lecture, a fierce controversy broke out between Charles Villiers Stanford and Sharp as to when a folk song was a folk song. Stanford became heated and rude as Sharp demonstrated with his customary skill the distinction between 'the genuine folk-tune and the composed song', and although Sharp proved his point such internecine conflict was damaging to the wider interests of the society, in particular the chances of having folk song put into the school curricula, for Stanford operated for the Board of Education.

The success of the Folk Song Society in centralising the efforts of field workers encouraged the formation in 1904 of the Irish Folk-Song Society, and in 1908 of a Welsh society, and also led to the establishment of the Folk Dance Society, also largely due to the enthusiasm of Cecil Sharp. Sharp had his attention drawn to the dance by witnessing in 1899 a Morris dance in the village of Headington, near Oxford. In 1911 the first Stratford-upon-Avon Summer School of Folk-Song and Dance was held, lasting a month and attended by more than 200 people from all over the world. Cecil Sharp was not the first in this field, though his renown and authority eclipsed others, such as Mary Neal, who died in 1944 and who at one time worked closely with him, taking bands of London working girls to different parts of the country to demonstrate the liveliness of folk dance. It is ironical that Sharp, forgetting his 1906 axioms on the desirability of letting the fittest folk music survive through a process of natural selection, should have broken with Miss Neal on this very point; he maintained that the dances should be maintained in exactly the form in which they had been gathered, while Miss Neal considered that since the dances had arrived at that point in time by evolution, the process should be allowed to continue.

Throughout the period there were two divergent views on the value of folk music. Was it there, as Parry considered, for the benefit of middle-class patronage, or was there poetic virtue in rural idiom and integrity of especial power in country life? Were the enthusiasts merely in thrall to nostalgia, engrossed in a vision of country life that had never borne any relation to the truth?

The musical world was split. The traditional composers believed that music was really the business of foreigners and that the only true style came from tagging along in the footsteps of Brahms. The professional musicians were either church or university orientated—both Stanford and Parry were professors at Oxford—and were, apart from their credentials in music, clever men. Stanford in particular was a brilliant teacher, and amongst his pupils were Vaughan Williams, John Ireland, Herbert Howells and Gustav Holst.

Although Stanford was a key figure in the folk-song movement it must be remembered that he was Irish, not English, that his work was full of Irish tunes but not English, and that he

To many, the folk-song movement was associated with the arch and pretentious, as portrayed in 'An Idyll'.

edited a large collection of Irish folk music between 1902 and 1905. Another leading musician involved in the folk-music revival was Percy Grainger, who was initially thrust right into the European mainstream by studying at Frankfurt. As a folk-song collector and editor Grainger was scrupulous, but in his own work he felt obliged to modify the music for performance. Nevertheless, he wrote a handful of vivacious works with a folk-music flavour that enjoyed public acclaim—these include *Mock Morris*, *Molly on the Shore*, *Country Gardens*, and a passacaglia, *Green Bushes*. In terms of times played, *Country Gardens*, beloved of infant-school mistresses for assembly and marching children round a classroom, must hold the record for any piece of folk-sounding music before the present-day revival.

An engaging and distinctive personality, Grainger was a pioneer in the use of recording machines for field work, and was always eager to share his discoveries with colleagues—it was he who gave Delius the tune 'Brigg Fair' to work his chromatic wiles on.

Grainger was not an academic who felt obliged to alter folk tunes because they were inartistic and did not fit in with the grand plan, but an extremely talented composer who knew and felt the quirkishness, the angularity, and the mode-like quality of the tunes that he had collected, and amplified them. He, although an Australian, was desperate to preserve the Englishness of the tunes he harmonised and set before the wider public, and he was one of the first to discard Italian instructions from the scores of his compositions and substitute homely English. Another one of the 'Frankfurt gang' who threw himself into folk music was Henry Balfour Gardiner, known almost solely by a work very much in the Grainger style, *Shepherd Fennel's Dance*, played at the Promenade Concerts in 1911.

If the folk music revival did nothing more, it did produce a brace of exhilarating orchestral works that have a unique English-ness, as illustrative of place as the Cockney music-hall songs. It also produced a distinctive genius—not Vaughan Williams, who would have been a great composer whatever the circumstances—who was dependent on folk music for his life-blood: known by two orchestral rhapsodies and a handful of songs, almost his total output, George Butterworth is an example of a man who was fired by the example of Cecil Sharp and his colleagues, and produced work that transdcended the genre.

While he was still a schoolboy at Eton, a barcarolle by Butter-worth was performed. He went up to Trinity College, Oxford, in 1904 to read classics and prepare for a legal career, but acquain-tance with members of the folk-song movement deflected him into music, first as a *Times* music critic then into teaching. Butterworth was very keen on Morris dancing, and collected songs in Sussex before writing his two masterpieces, *The Banks of Green Willow* and *A Shropshire Lad*. These were performed shortly before World War I, in which Butterworth was killed on the Somme.

Did the folk-music revival do anything more than fire talented composers such as Balfour Gardiner, Grainger, Butterworth, and Vaughan Williams? Delighted as the public was with their works, this was the concert-going public, and the classics of the move-ment were of no more concern to the man in the street than Bach or Beethoven. Sincerity, simplicity and serenity were, said Vaughan Williams, the elements of greatness, and all these characteristics were seen by him to belong to folk song. They were also qualities that characterise his own folk-inspired work— *On Wenlock Edge*, the *Norfolk Rhapsody*, and the music to *The Wasps*—and some of the early music of Gustav Holst. Did sincerity, simplicity and serenity interest the mass public? The answer must be 'no'. For sincerity they substituted ballad sentimentality and the cynical posturings of the balladmongers, for simplicity the arch and the feeble-minded, and as for serenity, this was a concept way out of their reach.

Looking back in 1934, Vaughan Williams did not consider that the battle had been lost: 'When about twenty-five years ago Cecil Sharp collected and published his new discoveries in English folk song he had in mind the ordinary man, the "divine average" of Whitman. And it is the ordinary man for whose musical salvation the folk-song will be responsible.' Perhaps there was a point when the outcome of the conflict was in doubt. Certainly educational authorities were not slow to appreciate that folk music could be incorporated into scholastic programmes, but teachers, themselves not experts, were not able to differentiate between genuine folk song and the imitation. To them it was all one, whether it was 'The Skye Boat Song' (fake) or 'The Jolly Miller' (genuine), and it was certainly not their job to continue the controversy between Stanford and Sharp as to what constituted a folk song, immaterial whether there was a specific number of 'tune families' embracing all the repertoire of folk song (it was a shock to some collectors when they realised that one of the most pristine of folk songs, 'Brigg Fair', was a 'decadent' version of what is known as the 'Lazarus' air).

It was Cecil Sharp the name, and sharp the nature. He was anxious to find the clear-cut, the untrammelled, the unspoilt. But this was difficult when the distinction between composition and performance was fuzzy, and there was a good deal of heart-searching when an ageing performer of some long-lost gem sang the same words to tunes that varied with each rendering. At what stage did a tune become 'corrupt' and 'decadent'? Could it be that the singers discovered during the last decade of the last century and the first decade of this were so contaminated by contact with town and city that their wares were suspect?

Members of the Folk Song Society had to face this as best they could. They also had another problem. What were they to do about the urban folk songs, industrial work songs that dated back to the early days of the industrial revolution? There was more reluctance to concern oneself with the products of mill and factory, such as 'The Bury New Loom' first recorded in print in 1804, or 'The Colliers' Rant', published in 1793. Collectors were easier with lyrics dealing with the round of the seasons and rustic revels than a train of miners' grievances, and were thankful that the songs of the urban proletariat dealt with specific incidents and lacked universal appeal. There was no future in keeping them going, as the broadside printers did with country songs. (For every country folk singer there were probably half a dozen professional ballad singers in the towns warbling 'The Foggy-foggy Dew'.)

The general public was suspicious of folk song, of its being foisted on it for its own good. None of the foundation members of the Folk Song Society was working-class; the middle class was addressing inferiors across a chasm. Folk dancing was eternally risible, and still is, and there are few, country and town people alike, to whom forgotten rituals mean anything. The only way in which folk dancing has percolated down is in children's games, and, similarly, certain of the devices of folk song exist in the chants and rhythms of children's play songs. Perhaps this is how it should be, for much folk music was for use rather than entertainment, most clearly seen in sea shanties where the rhythms fit in with the movements of sailors at work. In agricultural work, song was used as a co-ordinator when duties involving numbers of men were carried out; in work where both men and women were present, the saucy song, one of the most important categories, was used as a catalyst. Not surprisingly, the country people of the Edwardian period, a section of the population diminishing in number and importance, wondered what relevance folk songs had for them when they were perfectly satisfied with easily accessible music-hall ditties and shop ballads. A minority entertainment form is accepted only when there is no alternative;

there were far too many alternatives for the Edwardian masses.

There was one revival of traditional melody that triumphed—the carol. Early in the nineteenth century this had gone into decline, and although antiquarians tried to preserve it there was a good chance of this medieval form going completely under, more so than Tudor or Stuart forms, for there were always madrigal societies and always someone somewhere who had a harpsichord and played the old music on it. The High Church movement was largely responsible for the Victorian interest in the carol; in 1853 *Carols for Christmastide* was published, followed by *Christmas Carols Old and New* (1865). The formation of the Folk Song Society sparked off more enthusiasm, and in 1900 *The Cowley Carol Book* was published, which included a number of foreign tunes. The folk-song collectors, searching in obscure corners of university libraries and browsing through piles of old music, found new material, and disinterred a genuine folk-carol in 'The Holly and the Ivy'.

Perhaps the carol is the only musical form where all are united—scholars, musicologists, church people, and the public. The carol was wanted to fill out Christmas, and it was immediately accepted. It satisfied a long-felt need; folk music did not.

It is inconceivable that anything of value goes out of circulation for long. Folk songs and pseudo-folk songs kept their place in society at a humble level, sung by children in schools with their words appropriately changed, until the time was ripe for the genuine article to emerge. This has happened in the present age. Coincident with this has been a revival amongst the young of Tudor and Stuart music, and often—as with the collectors and enthusiasts of the Edwardian age—folk music and old art music have been taken up by the same people. Class mobility has broken down the barrier between those who were trying to push folk music on to their social inferiors and those who were being pushed. As in most other spheres, something that is found for oneself is treated with much more love and care than something that is foisted on one with the instruction that it is good for one. Folk music is not medicine, but so it seemed to the Edwardian masses; the ingredients were insufficiently sweetened for their taste, and they did not like the writing on the label.

CHAPTER ELEVEN

THE COMING OF RAGTIME

THE EDWARDIANS WERE not acquainted with jazz at all, but they were with its precursor, ragtime. This was perhaps the most important genre in Edwardian popular music if one is looking for a guide-line to future events, and it arrived almost impercepceptibly. By the time the critics raged against it, ragtime had established itself.

Ragtime was music for the young, who were dissatisfied and contemptuous of ballads and the *schmaltz* of musical comedy. In particular the young wanted something lively to dance to, and the moribund state of English ballroom dancing was responsible for the whole-hearted way in which ragtime was greeted. There was also a move in dancing away from formal steps towards a walk, and in America at the turn of the century there were a large number of new dances including the bunny hug, the turkey trot, the grizzly bear, the crab step, the kangaroo dip, and the horse trot. Some of these flourished for a few months, and then died, but there was one dance, taken from the negroes, that established itself in America and Europe—the cake-walk.

This dance was done by two opposing lines of dancers, men on one side, women on the other, and each line advanced towards the other line, heads down, until nearly touching, then all bent their heads back and retreated in time to the music. In essence, it was a social dance, a type of square dance, but the music had a novel element—syncopation—and the distinctive rhythm was well-suited to words with a contemporary flavour.

The cake-walk was a direct result of the tendency of American negro bands to jazz-up marches. Negro marching bands were in existence prior to 1881, when more than a dozen took part in the procession in New Orleans to mourn the death of the anti-slavery advocate President Garfield, and it is believed that the transition from brass band to jazz band occurred around 1890. To the Edwardians the cake-walk was synonymous with ragtime simply because knowledge was limited.

The first published piece of ragtime is believed to be 'New Coon in Town', published in 1884 and sub-titled 'Banjo Imitation'. The piano was a key instrument in early ragtime, because it was able to exploit banjo techniques; one piano could do all that three or four banjos could do, and do it better. The first piece that had the word 'ragtime' in the title was 'Ma Ragtime Baby', written by Fred Stone and published in 1893, and the word caught on. 'Turkey in the Straw' (1896), often found in books of American square dances, was called a 'Ragtime Fantasie', and in 1897 Thomas Million Turpin (died 1922) published his 'Harlem Rag'. This was followed by 'Ragtime Nightmare' and 'St Louis Rag'. Owing to Turpin's influence, many ragtime players became famous overnight, among them Scott Joplin (1869–1917), often believed to be the originator of piano ragtime.

Joplin's 'The Original Rags' was a medley of rags, published in 1897, and in 1899 he followed this with what became a rag classic, 'Maple Leaf Rag'. Altogether Joplin wrote about fifty rags and tunes flavoured with the idiom, but he was suspect to most of the other negro composers because he wrote 'on paper' as opposed to composing at the piano. The tendency today is to take these turn-of-the-century rags at breakneck speed, though it is evident that at the time they were performed at a moderate pace. Indeed, Joplin often placed 'Do Not Play Fast' at the head of his sheet music. In 1906 Jelly Roll Morton composed 'King Porter Stomp', a forerunner of true jazz compositions, and about that time a number of ragtime bands were built up in the United States to cater for the craze, though the word 'jazz', initially spelled 'jass', was not to arise for another decade.

Most of these developments were unknown to the Edwardians.

All they knew was that the cake-walk was different. One of the best known of the cake-walk songs was:

> When we are married we'll have sausages for tea
>   Sausages for tea
>   Sausages for tea;
> When we are married we'll have sausages for tea
>   Sausages for you and me.

Nothing could be further removed from the insipidity of the royalty ballad, and the lyrics were far more akin to those of the music-hall song, though the cake-walk words had an off-beat piquancy, a relish in the almost hypnotic repetition of phrases, that was rare in the music hall. There were also memories of nigger minstrelsy and echoes of the 'coon-song' of the 1880s. The cake-walk was the first indication of the powerful role negro music was to play in the twentieth century.

Many dance halls ignored the cake-walk, but even excepting that dance there were changes. Waltzes were still immensely popular, but although at fashionable balls and assemblies the fast waltz—what is known today as the old-tyme waltz—was *de rigueur*, in the dance halls the tempo was slowed right down. The waltz became an intimate, sexually motivated dance, not an exercise in calisthenics. A sign of the future was the popularity of a 'walking dance', the Boston, which appeared about 1909, and in 1911 a new tune by Irving Berlin was heard, 'Alexander's Ragtime Band'.

Dancing at this time was a widespread pastime. 1911 saw the first Chelsea Arts Ball with fifteen-shilling tickets changing hands at £5, and in the same year 4,000 people turned up for the Shakespeare Ball, with music supplied by the Corelli-Windeatt Band, numbering 130. This orchestra and the leading dance band of the day, Herr Gottlieb's Viennese Orchestra (all British, despite the name), would soon be desperately out of date, for the Irving Berlin tune ushered in new ragtime numbers and new dancing techniques.

Ragtime needed a respectable platform, and found it in the revue, a type of entertainment that had gone down well at the

THE POETRY OF MOTION, 1909
The "Borston."

*The Boston revolution-
ised the dance-music
world.* (Punch)

*Despite the introduc-
tion of the Boston and
ragtime, waltzes still
held sway, fortified by
new tunes from the
musical-comedy reper-
toire. The dance floor
was still basically a
place for boy to meet
girl.* (Woman's
World)

London Hippodrome in 1912 and was a revamping of the old-time burlesque, combining pantomime and variety. In the summer of 1913 the show *Hullo Ragtime* met with astonishing success at the Hippodrome, and was seen by 400,000 people, tired of the long-lasting mellifluity of musical comedy. *Hullo Ragtime* ushered in a brand new kind of stage show, and included three ragtime numbers that were immediately to establish themselves in the canon of popular music—'Waiting for the Robert E. Lee', 'Row, Row, Row', and the tune that created most furore, 'Hitchy Koo'. As a result of the success of *Hullo Ragtime* and other 1913 ragtime-orientated revues such as *Hullo Tango*, *Keep Smiling*, *Eightpence a Mile* (which introduced 'That Syncopated Boogie Boo'), and *Kill That Fly*, seventy-five different revues were soon running in the provinces, dealing a harsh and often fatal blow to travelling troupes of musical-comedy players.

Ragtime was all that the respectable musical press hated about popular music, and an editorial in the *Musical News* was typical of many. 'Hitchy Koo' was

> the last word in aimless, brainless rottenness. But the rag-time will soon have its day over here, thank goodness, and we shall return to the ditty of the type of 'I wonder if you miss me sometimes', maudlin enough in its way but dealing with genuine and homely sentiment. These sort of songs which appeal intensely to the humbler classes do not vary in their sentiments. They are all about the amours of a 'fellow and a girl' but the love is true and the words perfectly free from offence.

The Times was more sensible: 'There is surely nothing unhealthy or lascivious in the music itself—indeed, its very vigour and rhythm must have a stimulating effect on the popular musical mind.' In March 1913 the *Observer* published an amusing poem:

> At dawn beneath my casement,
>   Scrubbing the area stairs,
> The boot-boy in the basement
>   Is whistling rag-time airs.

> At breakfast, while I'm eating,
>   A German band outside
> With unction keeps repeating
>   The latest 'Wedding Glide',
> Where'er I go, what e'er I do,
>   I can't escape from 'Hitchy Koo'.
> Pursued as by a pixy
>   By each infectious air,
> I 'Want to Be in Dixie'
>   When everybody's there!
> Though 'Honolulu-looing'
>   I've done my best to shun,
> What 'Everybody's Doing'
>   I cannot leave undone!
> The subtle spell I can't withstand
>   Of 'Alexander's Ragtime Band'!

Typical of quintessential ragtime was 'He'd Have to Get Under—Get Out and Get Under', sung in the Hippodrome revue *Hullo Tango*. In many ways it is the American equivalent of the London music-hall narrative song, but, unlike most of the British numbers, it was contemporary. Realistic in tone as were many of the pseudo-Cockney music-hall hits, there was a Victorian veneer about them with stereotyped mother-in-law and disgruntled-husband situations. Thoroughly modern references appealing especially to young men and women were characteristic of the ragtime numbers, and it was difficult for anyone to imagine the old-timers of the music hall being mentally or physically equipped to rap out the lyrics of time ragmusic, such as the following:

Verse: Johnny O'Connor bought an automobile,
           He took his sweetheart for a ride one Sunday.
           Johnny was togged up in his best Sunday clothes,
           She nestled close to his side.
           Things went just dandy 'til he got down the road,
           Then something happen'd to the old machin'ry.
           That engine got his goat,

HE'D HAVE TO GET UNDER— GET OUT AND GET UNDER.

(To fix up his Automobile.)

WRITTEN BY

Grant Clarke and Edgar Leslie.

COMPOSED BY

MAURICE ABRAHAMS.

FEATURED IN THE

HIGHLY SUCCESSFUL REVUE

HULLO, TANGO!

HIPPODROME, LONDON.

Book by
MAX PEMBERTON AND ALBERT P. de COURVILLE.

Lyrics by   Music by
George Arthurs.   Louis Hirsch.

Produced by NED WAYBURN.

Sung with Immense Popularity

by GERALD KIRBY.

Photo by Foulsham & Banfield Ltd

COPYRIGHT.   PRICE 2/- NET.

London:
FRANCIS, DAY & HUNTER,
142, CHARING CROSS ROAD, W.C.
NEW YORK:
THE MAURICE ABRAHAMS' MUSIC COMPANY, 1570, BROADWAY.

Copyright MCMXIII. {In Great Britain and Colonies (except Canada and Australasia) by Francis, Day & Hunter. {In United States of America by The Maurice Abrahams Music Company.

'He'd Have to Get Under—Get Out and Get Under', one of the
pioneering ragtime songs.

Off went his hat and coat,
Everything needed repairs.
Chorus: He'd have to get under, get out and get under
To fix his little machine.
He was just dying
To cuddle his queen,
But ev'ry minute
When he'd begin it,
He'd have to get under, get out and get under,
Then he'd get back at the wheel.
A dozen times they'd start to hug and kiss—
And then the darn'd old engine it would miss,
And then he'd have to get under, get out and get
under,
And fix up his automobile.

Ragtime brought an absolutely new sort of music to British audiences, and there was a massive market for exploitation by the Americans. The dance revival in Britain was paralleled by the same thing in the United States, but on an enlarged scale. Dance mania spread across the States, and the record companies could hardly keep up with the demand for dance music, especially for ragtime. In 1912 there were only three American record manufacturers, in 1914 there were nine, in 1915 there were twenty-seven, and in 1916 there were more than sixty. Naturally World War I curbed the dance-music scene in Britain, though dance music and ragtime still flourished to some extent during the war (together with a revival of musical comedy).

At the same time as ragtime made itself known there arose a craze for exotics and curios of all kinds, corresponding with upheavals in the whole structure of society. The suffragette movement, with bombings, arson, and attacks on property, was providing a problem for the government, a problem with which it was at a loss to deal, and the arts were being turned turtle by a variety of manifestations—the impact of the Russian ballet and the Post-Impressionist painters, and what was thought to be the fragmentation of music by Schoenberg and Stravinsky. It seemed to many that everything that was represented by the Victorians was being cast overboard, a revolt by the young and under-privileged against their elders. Trades union membership boomed, strikes were frequent, women wanted the vote; the twentieth century, exemplified by the invasion of ragtime, had arrived with a bang.

Another instance of the appeal of the new was a further import from the Americas, the tango, which hit London with almost the same impact as ragtime. Created by the African slaves in Haiti and Cuba in the eighteenth century, the tango was as respectable as ragtime was reprehensible. Dancers were bidden to walk, glide and sway with no movement of the shoulders; legs were straightened or relaxed but rarely bent, and the woman should move with the 'sinuous grace of a tiger'.

One of the results of the tango boom was the 'Thé Tango', and exclusive hotels such as the Waldorf and the Cecil ran Tango Tea Dances, Prince's Restaurant initiated a Tango Club, and books were written by society writers on the etiquette of giving Thés

New dance music such as the tango brought a change of venue, and typical of the intimate night spots was Murray's, founded in 1913.
(Wonderful London)

Tangos at home—small tables should be placed around the dance floor which should preferably be parquet; a drawing-room offered quite enough space for the dancers to manoeuvre, for it was not a common dance like the Veleta, so popular in the industrial towns of the north. The tango was genteel yet sensuous, and to the late Edwardian mind this was an ideal combination.

Another dance from America was the maxixe, derived from a Brazilian urban dance that combined a sort of polka with the native habañera, and although there was a fad for the maxixe it was not widespread. The maxixe bided its time and nearly half a century later it reappeared, with great success, as the samba.

The most important of the dances that appeared just before World War I was the foxtrot, first danced in America in 1914. This, with the quickstep and the waltz, became the standard dance-hall dance for fifty years. The modified walk kept going when the tangos and the sambas, jive and jitterbug, lost their impact and were regarded as occasional dances.

The coming of ragtime involved musicians in aesthetic discussions about syncopation, and those serious musicologists who welcomed the verve and vigour argued that it was nothing new and could be found in the acknowledged masterpieces of the past, in, for example, Bach's Concerto for Two Violins. Many composers used ragtime as a basis for valid compositions; an early practitioner was Debussy whose suite *Children's Corner* (1906–8) included 'The Golliwog's Cakewalk'. In 1918 Stravinsky wrote his *Ragtime for Eleven Instruments*, following it in 1919 with *Piano Rag Music*.

This use of Afro-American forms was regarded with horror by the purists, who would have been aggrieved to have learned that as early as the mid-nineteenth century the American white composer Louis Moreau Gottschalk (1829–69)—who had studied in Europe and enjoyed the acquaintance of Chopin and Berlioz— had composed a dance piece called 'Le Bamboula' in the authentic cake-walk rhythm which he had picked up in Louisiana when a boy.

It is therefore not surprising that the cake-walk appeared on the scene in the opening decade of the twentieth century—more surprising, perhaps, that it had not appeared before. This was due to the American equivalent of music hall, vaudeville, taking a lead from Europe and ignoring its own rich heritage, little realising that Afro-American music was to be the multi-purpose urban folk music of the twentieth century.

Edwardian popular music differs from Victorian popular music in a number of ways. There was an increasing emphasis on music for the young and on music orientated to modern life; dance music was more broadly based, and appealed to those who went to dances not so much for the pleasures involved in dancing but to meet people of the opposite sex. The Edwardians were apprehensive about the future, and escaped into a never-never world represented by *The Merry Widow* and other operettas and musical comedies.

One of the most significant aspects of the scene was the growing influence of American music, from *The Belle of New York*, through the all-negro show *In Dahomey*, to the Boston, the tango, and ragtime. Impresarios realised that they had to take the American market into consideration when promoting homespun musical comedy, and parochial products such as Edward German's *Tom Jones*, expertly carpentered as it was, could not hope to do well in the United States.

The appeal to the mass audience was also evident in music hall, and with the accent on bigger and better music halls the localised and the topical were resolutely out (with the exception of pseudo-Cockney, the *lingua franca* of vaudeville). Only the smaller music halls could afford to tailor their presentations to the local audience.

And all the entertainment media were looking at the effect of the gramophone. Except with the prestige discs, the song was more important than the singer; certain performers whose voices came over well sang under a variety of names. The increase in record sales forced down the sale of sheet music, and although a composer or lyric writer could make a fortune overnight the old-fashioned ballad composer could no longer reckon on a safe income from sheet-music sales (if only because traditional ballads could not be slotted into the two minutes of the popular record and there was therefore no tie-up between a record and sheet music).

There was very little proletarian participation in popular music except in the north of England where amateur choirs and industrial brass bands were still going strong. Despite the efforts of enthusiasts to encourage a revival of folk song amongst those whom they consciously thought of as the lower orders, folk song and dance remained a minority pursuit. Amateur participation in popular music is epitomised by the banjo. The banjo was a middle-class instrument—in England, though not in America—undemanding and ideal for the inexpert.

This might be the final summing-up of Edwardian popular music—undemanding and ideal for the inexpert. In retrospect it is perhaps surprising that the composers of the time gave us so many delicious melodies, transcending their environment as if aware that a new age of popular music was to break upon them.

APPENDIX

Extracts from Edwardian Record Catalogues

10-inch   NICOLE DISC RECORDS   2/6 each

CORNET.

Our Cornet Solos and Duets are marvellously executed and render the true Cornet tone.

5238	Birds of the Forest Polka	Cornet Duet	Leggett aud Night'ngale
5237	Friendly Rivals Polka	"	Leggett and Nightingale
5240	Merry Swiss Girls Polka	"	Leggett and Nightingale
5241	Twin Brothers	"	Leggett and Nightingale
5239	Two Little Finches	"	Leggett and Nightingale
5242	Two Postillions	"	Leggett and Nightingale
5224	Alice, where art Thou ?	Cornet Solo	Charles Leggett
5211	Flight of Ages	"	Charles Leggett
5226	Genevieve	"	Charles Leggett
5212	I'll Sing Thee Songs of Araby	"	Charles Leggett
5213	Il Bacio (*Arditi*)	"	Charles Leggett
5210	Killarney	"	Charles Leggett
7704	La Lune de Miel (*F. Ligner*)	"	N. Bizet
5227	Mary	"	Charles Leggett
5228	Mary of Argyle	"	Charles Leggett
7706	Mimma (*F. Leroux*)	"	N. Bizet
7701	Myrto (*A. S. Petit*)	"	N. Bizet
5198	Quand tu Chantes (with Band)	"	H.M. Irish Guards
5223	Queen of the Earth	"	Charles Leggett
5494	Rosita (with Band accpt.)	"	Charles Leggett
5225	Solveigs Lied (*Grieg*)	"	Charles Leggett
5715	Trumpeter of Sakkingen	"	Charles Leggett
	(Behuet' Dich Gott, es wär' so schön gewesen)		
5216	Violets	Cornet Solo	Charles Leggett
5161	When all was Young "Faust" (Band accpt.)		Charles Leggett

FLUTE.

5318	Fantasia (*Nicholson*)	Flute Solo	H. Wilson
5320	The Wren		H. Wilson

ORCHESTRA BELLS.

Everyone hearing these records is charmed by their sweet effect and no record collection is complete without them.

5754	Fun in the Cornfields	Orchestra Bells	Madame Paula
	(with Orchestra and effects)		
5668	Home, Sweet Home	"	Madame Paula
5712	Moonlight Da ce (with Orchestra)		Madame Paula
5685	Moonlight Dance (with Piano accpt. and		
	Clog effect)	Orchestra Bells	Madame Paula
5490	On Emancipation Day	"	Jas. I. Lent
5667	Silver Bells March	"	Madame Paula
5711	Silver Bells March (with Orch.)	"	Madame Paula
5491	The Pansy and the Butterfly	"	Jas. I. Lent

PIANO.

5689	Amoretten Tanz	Piano	F. D. Wood
7647	Gavotte Princesse (*D. Bernieux*)	"	By the Composer
5669	Morgenblaetter Waltz	"	F. D. Wood
5581	Pierrette (Chaminade)	"	F. D. Wood
7648	Polonaise de Chopin	"	D. Bernieux
7646	Valse Brillante (*D. Bernieux*)	"	By the Composer

Please do not give the above 10 n. numbers if 7in. size is required.

10-inch   NICOLE DISC RECORDS   2/6 each

PICCOLO.

These selections are standard favourites and demonstrate Mr.
Wilcocke's brilliant execution and technique.

5332	Danse des Satyrs	Piccolo	Jas. Wilcocke
5334	Daybreak in the Forest	„	Jas. Wilcocke
5130	Deep Blue Sea (with Band accpt.)	„	Jas. Wilcocke
5335	Echoes of the Forest	„	Jas. Wilcocke
5201	Picaroon (with Band accpt.)	„	H.M. Irish Guards
5319	Scherzo Brilliante	„	Jas. Wilcocke
5111	Sylvia	„	Jas. Wilcocke
5333	The Captive Bird	„	Jas. Wilcocke
5336	The Linnet	„	Jas. Wilcocke

POST HORN.

5464   Post Horn Galop (Band accpt.) Post Horn   W. J. Price

VIOLIN.

5686   Cavatina (*Raff*)   Violin   L. Amando

VIOLONCELLO.

5802   Broken Melody (*August Van Beine's*) 'Cello   Charles Longwait

XYLOPHONE.

This instrument is becoming more and more popular and we find
the records greatly appreciated.

5774	American Belle	Xylophone Solo	C. Penner
5690	Irish Jig	„	C. Penner
5710	Kentucky Patrol (with band)	„	C. Penner
5709	Le Centaur „ „	„	C. Penner
5665	Le Centaur	„	C. Penner

WHISTLING.

Mr. Capper is one of the cleverest whistlers to be found and the Records here
reproduced are excellent.

5748	Carmena	Whistling Solo	Charles Capper
5729	Il Bacio	„	Charles Capper
5666	Jolly Fellows Waltz	„	Albert Whelan
5757	L'Ardita (with Orch. accpt.)	„	Charles Capper
5749	Les Folies Polka	„	Charles Capper
5756	Should He Upbraid (Orch. accpt.)	„	Charles Capper
5537	Whistling Rufus	„	Signor Guido Gialdini

SONGS.

5377	A Farmyard Medley	Quartette	American Comedy Four
5372	A Gentleman of France	Baritone	Harrison Brockbank
5724	A Hundred Fathoms Deep	Bass	Walter G. Webber
5719	A Little Boy called Taps (Band)	Baritone	Hamilton Hill
5762	A Little Silver Ring (Chaminade)	„	Edgar Coyle
5312	A May Morning	Soprano	Miss Kate Cove
5470	A Nice Old Maid	Humorous	W. W. Whitlock
5249	A Nigger's Laughing Song	Coon Song	Wilson Hallett

Please do not give the above 10in. numbers if 7in. size is required.

10-inch NICOLE DISC RECORDS 2/6 each

SONGS—*Continued.*

5295	A Sprig of Rosemarie, "Princess of Kensington"	Baritone	Randall Jackson
5468	Alice, where art Thou ?	Tenor	Wilfrid Virgo
5448	All I said was Ha ! Ha ! Ha !	Comic	W. W. Whitlock
5605	All the little ducks went quack	Humorous	Alf. Gordon
5328	And his day's work was done	Humorous	Alf. Gordon
5608	Annie Laurie	Baritone	W. L. Cockburn
5563	Any Rags	Comic	Pete Hampton
5009	'Arry 'Arry 'Arry		Fred T. Daniels
5371	At my Lady's Feet, " Lady Molly "	Barit.	Edgar Coyle
5698	At the Bottom of the Deep Blue Sea	Bass	Peter Dawson
	A new song modelled on that of "The Diver."		
5205	At the Seaside	Comic	Will Randall
5134	Auld Lang Syne	Baritone	Ian Colquhoun
5353	Ave Maria (*Bach-Gounod*)	Soprano	Miss Mabel Medrow
5435	Because	Baritone	Leonard Russell
	A good song charmingly rendered.		
5543	Bedelia, " The Orchid "	„	Lloyd Morgan
5072	Beyond	Mezzo-Soprano	Miss Lilian Doreen
5566	Biddy Aroo	Bass	Bernard Dudley
5177	Bill Bailey, won't you please come home ?		Pete Hampton
5593	Blue Bell (Orch. accpt)	Baritone	Geo. Warfield
5573	Blue Bell	„	Steve Porter
5741	Bombay on the Nile (Orch. accpt.)		Walter Passmore
5188	Boys of the Old Brigade (Band accpt.),,		Ian Colquhoun
5042	Buying a House (Leno)	Comic	Fred. T. Daniels
5622	By the Shores of the Mediterranean	Barit	Lloyd Morgan
5219	Can't you Take my Word (Ford)	Comic	Will Deller
5540	Cavalleria Rusticana—Siciliana	Tenor	Romeo Berti
5732	Charlie is my Darling (Scotch)	Soprano	Miss A. Robertson
5572	Come, Come, Caroline (Arthur Roberts)		Fred. T. Daniels
5471	Come under my new Gamp	Comic	W. W. Whitlock
5392	Comin' thro' the Rye	Soprano	Miss Ghita Corri
5526	Consume them all, " St. Paul "	Sacred	Frank Arthur
5040	Cook who Cooks	Comic	Fred. T. Daniels
5070	Could you be True to Eyes of Blue ?		Miss Lilian Doreen
5004	Dear Home Land	Baritone	Edgar Coyle
5717	Down at the Old Bull and Bush (with Orchestra)	Serio Comic	C. Adams
5571	Down at the Old Bull and Bush	„	Miss Edith Manley
5550	Down the Vale	Baritone	Edgar Coyle
5623	Egypt	„	Lloyd Morgan
5549	Eileen Alannah	„	Edgar Coyle
5370	Even Bravest Heart " Faust "	„	Edgar Coyle
5575	Farewell, My Little Yo San	„	Hamilton Hill
5022	Fol-the-rol-lol (Lashwood)	Comic	Steve Porter
5813	For All Eternity	Bass	Peter Dawson
5600	For Love of You	„	Henry Drew
5541	Flower Song, " Carmen "	Tenor	Romeo Berti
5607	Gae Bring to Me a Pint o' Wine	Baritone	W. L. Cockburn
5728	Genevieve	Contralto	Miss E. Blanchard
5661	Geordie Mackinlish	Comic	A. Carmichael
5299	Golden Lilies	Baritone	Randall Jackson
5314	Good Bye (*Tosti*)	Soprano	Miss Kate Cove

Please do not give the above 10in. numbers if 7in. size is required.
9

7-inch   # NICOLE DISC RECORDS   **1/- each**

DANCE MUSIC—*Continued.*

4392	Oh! Sammy, Fig. 4	Lancers	Nicole Orchestra
4394	Oh! Sammy, Fig. 5 (1st half)	„	Nicole Orchestra
4395	Oh! Sammy, Fig. 5 (2nd half)	„	Nicole Orchestra
4397	Jollification, Fig. 1	Quadrille	Nicole Orchestra
4398	Jolification, Fig. 2	„	Nicole Orchestra
4399	Jolification, Fig. 3	„	Nicole Orchestra
4400	Jolification, Fig. 4	„	Nicole Orchestra
4401	Jolification, Fig. 5 (1st half)	„	Nicole Orchestra
4402	Jolification, Fig. 5 (2nd half)	„	Nicole Orchestra

DESCRIPTIVE SELECTIONS.

4407	Adventures at the Zoo	W. W. Whitlock
4408	Adventures on a Motor Car	W. W. Whitlock
4497	Battle of Mukden	Nicole Orchestra
4326	Bill Bailey's Wedding (with Bell effec's)	W. W. Whitlock
4525	Down South	Meistersingers Orchestra
4527	Song and Story (Concertina)	Percy Honri

INSTRUMENTAL.

BANJO.

4432	A Ragtime Episode	Banjo	Charles Rogers
3140	Coon Band Contest	„	Charles Rogers
3139	Darkies' Patrol	„	Charles Rogers
3502	Favourite March	„	Charles Rogers
3138	Hiawatha	„	Charles Rogers
4433	Nigger in a Fit	„	Charles Rogers
3142	Smokey Mokes	„	Charles Rogers
3504	The Coloured Major	„	Charles Rogers
3501	Whistling Rufus	„	Charles Rogers
4434	Yankee Doodle	„	Charles Rogers

CLARIONET.

4042	Comin' Thro the Rye	Clarionet	Alec Smith
3335	Rigoletto	„	Alec Smith
4044	The Last Rose of Summer (variations)	„	Alec Smith

CONCERTINA.

The selections played on the Concertina show what music can be obtained from an instrument which of late years has apparently fallen on evil times. Mr. Honri's execution is marvellous.

4528	Entry of Gladiators	Concertina	Percy Honri
4522	Popular Melodies	„	Percy Honri
4527	Song and Story (Humorous)	„	Percy Honri

CORNET.

Our Cornet Solos and Duets are marvellously executed and render the true Cornet tone.

4132	The Merry Swiss Girls Polka	Cornet Duet	Leggett and Nightingale
4131	The Two Little Finches	„	Leggett and Nightingale
4101	Alice, where art Thou?	Cornet Solo	Charles Leggett
7705	Bruxelles (*O. Batifort*)	„	N. Bizet
4091	Flight of Ages	„	Charles Leggett
4445	Genevieve	„	Charles Leggett
7703	Hylda (*J. Reynaud*)	„	N. Bizet
4092	I'll Sing Thee Songs of Araby	„	Charles Leggett
4142	Imperial Polka	„	C. Butterworth
4090	Killarney	„	Charles Leggett

Please do not give the above 7in. numbers if 10in. size is required.

SELECT BIBLIOGRAPHY

Agate, James. *Immoment Toys* (1945)
Bailey, L. *Edwardian Scrapbook* (1957)
Benson, E. F. *As We Were* (1930)
Booth, J. B. *Old Pink 'Un Days* (1924)
——. *The Days We Knew* (1943)
Burke, Thomas. *Nights in Town* (c 1916)
Closson, E. *History of the Piano* (1947)
Davey, H. *History of English Music* (1921)
Felstead, S. Theodore. *Stars Who Made the Halls* (1946)
Fergusson, Louis. *Old Time Music Hall Comedians* (1949)
Forbes-Winslow, D. *Daly's* (1944)
Forsyth, Cecil. *Music and Nationalism* (1911)
Gaisberg, F. W. *Music on Record* (1946)
Galloway, W. J. *Musical England* (1910)
Gelatt, R. *The Fabulous Phonograph* (1956)
Hibbert, H. G. *Fifty Years of a Londoner's Life* (1916)
Howes, Frank. *English Musical Renaissance* (1966)
——. *Folk Music of Britain* (1969)
Hughes, Gervase. *Composers of Operetta* (1962)
Laver, James. *Edwardian Promenade* (1958)
Lee, Edward. *Music of the People* (1970)
Lloyd, A. L. *Folk Song in England* (1967)
Lubbock, Mark. *Complete Book of Light Opera* (1962)
Mackerness, E. D. *Social History of English Music* (1964)

Mackinlay, Sterling. *Origin and Development of Light Opera* (1928)
MacQueen Pope, W. *Twenty Shillings in the Pound* (1948)
——. *The Gaiety* (1949)
——. *Nights of Gladness* (1950)
——. *The Melodies Linger On* (1951)
——. *Shirtfronts and Sables* (1953)
Mander, Raymond, and Mitchenson, Joe. *British Music Hall* (1965)
——. *Musical Comedy* (1969)
Nettel, Reginald. *Seven Centuries of Popular Song* (1956)
Nettl, Paul. *The Story of Dance Music* (1947)
Nowell-Smith, Simon (ed). *Edwardian England* (1964)
Orde-Hume, Arthur. *The Player Piano* (1970)
Pearsall, Ronald. *Edwardian Life and Leisure* (1973)
Pulling, Christopher. *They Were Singing* (1952)
Russell, John F., and Elliot, J. H. *The Brass Band Movement* (1936)
Rust, Frances. *Dance in Society* (1969)
Scholes, Percy A. *The Oxford Companion to Music* (1938)
——. *Mirror of Music 1844-1944* (1947)
Scott, Harold. *The Early Doors* (1925)
Short, Ernest. *Fifty Years of Vaudeville* (1946)
Short, Ernest, and Compton-Rickett, Arthur. *Ring Up the Curtain* (1938)
Stevens, Denis (ed). *A History of Song* (1960)
Titterton, W. R. *From Theatre to Music Hall* (1912)
Walker, Ernest. *Music in England* (1907)
Weatherly, Fred. *Piano and Gown* (nd)
White, Eric. *The Rise of Opera in England* (1951)
Willson Disher, M. *Winkles and Champagne* (1938)
——. *Fairs, Circuses and Music Halls* (1942)
Young, P. M. *The Musical Tradition* (1962)

Newspapers Periodicals and Magazines
Bystander
Cassell's Magazine
Daily Telegraph

The Era
Illustrated London News
Monthly Musical Record
Music Trades Record
Musical News
Musical Opinion
Musical Standard
Musical Times
Musical World
The Observer
Pall Mall Magazine
Pearson's Magazine
Punch
The Sketch
Sound Wave
The Strand
Talking Machine News
The Tatler
The Times
Woman at Home
Woman's World

Music-Hall stars at a 1912 Garden Party at which there were 20,000 guests. The Music Hall had become respectable; twenty years earlier, such a gathering would have been inconceivable.

INDEX